10/22/96

To Br...

my ...

fellow accom...

friend & otherwise

trouble maker. All the Best,

October 28, 1996

Naperville, Il.

AGENCY

by

Jay McNamara

Edited by
Cricket Pechstein

Possibilities
Press
1995

AGENCY

International Standard Book Number: 0-9646347-0-8

Library of Congress Catalog Card Number: 95-68807

First Edition, June 1995
Current Edition: 8 7 6 5 4 3 2 1

Printed and bound in the United States of America.
Jacket Design: Cricket Pechstein
Front Cover Artwork: Jere Pechstein
Book Design: Cricket Pechstein

Published in North America by Possibilities Press, P.O. Box 780866, Sebastian, Florida 32978-0866.

This book is dedicated to all those who strive in the advertising agency business.

Once more into the breach, dear friends, once more.

- Henry the Fifth

DAY 30

Burns & Cody Advertising Agency, New York City

Murphy hurtled down the back stairway of the agency, the rolled-up letter clutched in his outstretched hand like a sprinter's baton. His need was to make a hand-off, to rid himself of this missile of doom ... like a relay racer, except you've never seen a pudgy relay racer.

Why had they addressed the letter to him? True, he was the senior account man on the business, but something this earth-shaking should have been written directly to the chairman of the agency.

Fifteen years of dining in New York's finest restaurants was not the best training for his twelve floor dash. He leapt the last three steps to each floor landing, coming in like a fat duck to a pond, except you've never seen a disheveled duck. Each jump made a loud bang, his feet stinging from the impact, his flaming hair flopping against his forehead, the explosive gases generated from a lunch of sauerbraten and red cabbage releasing, rat-a-tat-tat. He might have choked himself, except that he wore his shirt unbuttoned, his tie loose, like a prep school boy fighting a dress code.

How could this have happened to him? He had just written an account update for the chairman saying that the Global business was in great shape. At the eighth floor landing he passed Clay Walker exiting the men's room.

"Hey, Murphy, what's your hurry? Your bookie close at six?"

Murphy sped down, dismissed Walker with a wave. They were sure to blame him. Say his judgment was shot, that he'd been on the account too long. Or worse — that he'd hidden problems from management. He spotted the number 5 on the landing, burst through the door into the creative department. He covered the short distance to Dennis O'Brien's office, ran past his secretary.

"Where is he, Evelyn?"

"You just missed him, he left ... What's with you? You should sit down."

"He couldn't have, it's only six." Murphy started for the elevator bank, looked back at her.

"He can't be here all the time, you know. It's his birthday. He's meeting his wife at La Côte Basque."

There was no one at the elevator bank. Murphy retraced his steps back into the stairwell, headed for the bottom. From the lobby he caught a glance of the creative director's curly blonde hair as O'Brien went through the revolving door.

"Dennis," he began gasping before he reached the street. It took him half a block to catch up. "Dennis, Dennis, wait till you hear." Murphy grabbed his arm and O'Brien stopped short.

"Malachy, what's going on?"

"It's Global! They've put us on notice. We have thirty days. It's unbelievable. I got this letter from Kreeger."

"Calm down, Malachy." O'Brien put his hand on Murphy's shoulder, took him by the elbow, like a policeman with a school child at a crossing, turned him back toward the agency. He waved at the security desk, went toward the elevators.

"Dennis, how? ..."

O'Brien held his hand up, turned and acknowledged a group of departing agency people. Murphy looked at O'Brien, dried the sweat from his face with the upper arm of his shirt, in the manner of John McEnroe in the heat of a match. Back at the fifth floor, O'Brien led Murphy past his secretary to his office.

"Oh, oh, should I call the restaurant?" She looked Murphy up and down. "Or a doctor?"

"Not yet, Evelyn. Murphy and I need to talk for a minute."

He pointed at a chair for Murphy, took an opposite one. "O.K., Malachy, let's hear this from the beginning ... Slowly."

Murphy unraveled the letter, wrinkled from his sweat. "I got this by messenger fifteen minutes ago. It doesn't say much."

> Dear Malachy,
> Effective today the agency is on 30 days notice
> in accordance with our contract.
> Sincerely,
> Jack Kreeger

"Didn't we get a good evaluation about a month ago?"

"As good as we've ever gotten. And, since then they bought the fall campaign. Everybody loved it. You were at the presentation."

"So, there's something screwy going on. Have you told the chairman about this?"

"Dennis, I haven't had time to tell anyone but you."

"That's good. We don't want to cause mass hysteria around here. I'll get in touch with the chairman. He can contact the brass at Global. There'll be an explanation, I'm sure. Meanwhile, where will you be?"

"I've got a plane to San Sebastian, a meeting with the Minister of Tourism tonight."

"Don't change your plans." O'Brien leaned toward the door of his office. "Evelyn, call the restaurant, see if my wife is there yet. Tell them I'll be a little late. And, find out where Brad Burns is. I have to talk to him, no matter what."

O'Brien stood up, led Murphy toward the door. "Don't panic, Malachy, we'll figure this out."

Outside the office, Murphy glanced back, seeking to be reassured. But, O'Brien's smile was gone, as fast as a sunny day turned dark by a passing cloud, replaced by a look of concern in his eyes. Murphy hunched his shoulders, put his hands in his pockets, turned and left.

. . .

O'Brien rubbed his eyes, walked across his office to his hammock and sat down. The hammock stretched across the part of his office unseen from the doorway. It was suspended between two hooks screwed into adjacent walls. He had not put the hammock in his office to be different. It was an economic use of space, something he had little of in his early days at the agency. Besides taking up minimum room, he found it to be a restful escape from the anxieties of the advertising business. It reminded him of peaceful views, open spaces and clean air, qualities not common to Madison Avenue. He found, once suspended above the anxieties strewn below, swinging in mid-air, he could think clearly. Each time he had changed offices, eight times in his fifteen years at the agency, he had taken the hammock with him. It had become a familiar object to his associates, a symbol of his personality to those that knew him best.

Evelyn leaned into the room. "Bran Burns is due in from London in about fifteen minutes. He'll be calling when he lands. I told Bea that it was important that he talk to you." She placed some ads on his table. "And your wife's just arrived at the restaurant. I told them to let her know you'd be late."

"Good." He leaned back, stretched out in the hammock, hands behind his head. The Global news didn't add up. As the biggest account in the agency, everyone kept an eye on it. Brad Burns was a personal friend of the airline's chairman, Haps

Corwin. O'Brien, himself, looked at every ad before it was taken to the client, was involved in every important presentation. Murphy had run the account smoothly for over five years. Murphy. He didn't look very good tonight. He was scared. Maybe he knew more than he was saying.

"Dennis, Brad Burns is on line one."

O'Brien reached for the portable phone at the bottom of the hammock. "Hi, Boss. I'm sorry to hit you right off the plane, but it's important."

"What's up, Dennis?"

"Murphy got a letter from Jack Kreeger at Global. It says we're on thirty days notice."

"What? I'm staggered. That can't be. I thought things were in ship shape ... I don't know Kreeger, he's the new advertising director, isn't he?"

"Right, he came over from sales. Not the smartest guy in the world, knows nothing about advertising."

Evelyn crossed the office and held a note in front of O'Brien, "Your wife is on line two." O'Brien waved her away.

"Look, Dennis, I'll try to get hold of Haps Corwin. I can't believe he wouldn't have told me if there was a problem. I thought everyone at the airline liked the work we've done."

"We won the *Adweek* Best Airline Advertising Award for 1993." O'Brien shifted his weight in the hammock.

"Well, there may be a couple of other factors at work here. The new president, Bill Swenson, is a guy we don't know yet. And, of course, their business is awful. They can hardly make their debt payments."

"What do you want me to do, Brad?"

"First, let's keep it quiet until we know the full story. Then we can decide what needs to be done. If this is for real I want you personally on top of our creative efforts for the next thirty days. I don't have to remind you that Global was one-third of our profits last year."

"I'm well aware of that, believe me. I'll wait till I hear from you."

O'Brien put the phone down and lifted himself from the hammock. "Evelyn, what's the message from my wife?"

"She's waiting for you at the restaurant. She didn't sound too happy."

"Call them again and tell them I'm on my way, which I am. I'll see you tomorrow."

"Good night and Happy Birthday again, even if you don't like hearing it."

She was right about that. Forty-one. At least it didn't have a five or a zero at the end of it. It wasn't exactly a milestone, like the last one. Then, he had drawn up an elaborate list of goals for himself. He began to tick them off in his mind, but stopped at the first one. He had failed to get a divorce.

. . .

Madison Avenue

The cabby wore a red fez. His name on the dashplate was a hodge-podge of consonants, unpronounceable to O'Brien. O'Brien thought of engaging the man in conversation, but the protective shield between the front and the back of the cab was an impediment. Instead, he looked at the sheet of paper in his lap, the one prepared daily by Evelyn, a list of the major problems facing the agency.

Actually, two lists: one for clients and one for people. Global, which had not been on the list for many months, was now number one of a total of seven client problems. He tried to focus on what had to be done for the airline, but his mind kept returning to his failure to get a divorce. Another year had slipped by and he'd been unable to resolve it.

It wasn't that he expected his marriage to improve. It was beyond fixing. The few times he'd gotten the nerve to broach the subject with Helen he'd been stalled by his inability to figure out how to deal with Tommy, how to explain to his son that nothing would change, when he knew it would once he'd moved out of the house. He didn't see as much of the boy now as he wanted to. What would it be like if he didn't live there?

The business of the agency pulled at him and demanded his attention. Being creative director absorbed his time, drained his energy. Helen didn't understand that at the agency he was closest to being himself. He made a promise he would deal with the problem. But, not tonight, not in one of the best restaurants in the world.

He went back to the sheet of paper, this time to the list dealing with people. At the top was Jeremy Gaines, along with a notation:

> Meeting with Chairman at 10:00 a.m. tomorrow
> to discuss Gaines investigation.

The cab jerked to a halt. Just enough rain had begun to fall to make the city's normally hazardous traffic dangerous.

He dreaded the Gaines meeting. The chairman would order that Gaines be fired. The situation was extraordinary, even in a business where bizarre behavior was commonplace. Yet, O'Brien understood what had happened and why it had happened. Gaines had been fingered by a new agency computer program, one that reviewed every personal expense account. Based on five years of back data, the machine highlighted deviations from normal expense behavior, whether it was a breakfast in Pittsburgh or a ride to the airport in Hong Kong. There were over eleven hundred norms established. In any given month, five to ten people around the agency worldwide network had to explain their variances.

In Gaines' case, the program had determined that his hotel bills showed excessive laundry and valet charges. The upshot had been a security department intercept of Gaines at his New York apartment upon his return from a trip to Miami. What they found was at the same time hilarious and pathetic to O'Brien.

He glanced out the window. A tiny woman, clinging to a huge red umbrella, was passing. It was the same woman O'Brien had observed several blocks earlier. The wind was strong. The woman was pulled forward by the umbrella, her feet skipping along the ground to keep up.

When the security people confronted Gaines, he had run into the street. The first of the two suitcases he was carrying spilled open. It was filled with freshly laundered clothing. Gaines' habit had been to take his laundry with him on trips, getting it done by the hotels at company expense. It was a first in the annals of agency expense account cheating. But, the second suitcase beat that. It was loaded with items from the hotel: towels, ashtrays, a bath robe, and a small framed picture. Gaines was nuts.

Which was not news to O'Brien. Gaines was also one of the two or three best copy writers in the agency, a writer whose fame placed him in demand in an industry whose only product was ideas. The same lunacy which led to Gaines' travel mania could synthesize ten pounds of research into one zinging headline.

O'Brien understood Gaines' laundry trick. A year earlier, Gaines had come to O'Brien's office to complain that the company's new family leave policy was unfair, since Gaines had no children, and never would have. Because Gaines was gay, the family program excluded him. He wanted the company to provide his with a benefit of equal value, extra vacation time, for example.

Gaines had a valid argument. But, O'Brien couldn't get the agency's executive committee to take the issue seriously, they being to-a-man, family men. O'Brien had stalled Gaines ever since and Gaines had reacted by developing his own benefit program, "Free laundry services for travelling executives." Fleecing the hotels must have been a logical next step to Gaines' way of thinking.

O'Brien looked at his Movado. He would be an hour late for dinner. This didn't bode well for the mood of the evening, already dour from the Global news and his birthday. Helen knew he hated his birthday. Yet, she had made reservations to celebrate it with conspicuous lavishness. He had put up an argument, but she had won. She usually did, reserving much of her considerable energy for their fights.

The worst part of the Gaines' case was that it would mar the brilliant man's reputation. In an age of public exposure, the amount of press was directly proportional to the oddity of the peccadillo. Gaines' case was sure to get plenty of exposure in the trade press, even if the general press overlooked it. The story was already around the agency, a source of great amusement.

Gaines would be gone. The chairman was a leader with a temperate hand, but he would not allow a public flaunting of the rules. O'Brien could understand that. What bothered him was the Gestapo, Big Brother mentality of the security department, little bureaucrats who thrived on exposing executives. O'Brien had calculated Gaines' laundry bills for a year, $1,200, a tiny percentage of the man's $275,000 compensation. He would point that out to the chairman, but it wouldn't have any weight.

"Here we are, sir," said the driver in perfect English.

"Where are you from?" said O'Brien.

"Originally, from Cairo, but I'm at Joulliard now."

"Joulliard?"

"Studying the cello, sir."

O'Brien smiled, shook his head. He doubled the size of his tip. "Good luck," he shouted as he darted through a heavier rain into La Côte Basque.

. . .

La Côte Basque Restaurant

The contrast between the dark, grimy, noisy street and the inside of the restaurant was complete. Aromas unique to fine French cuisine greeted you; paintings and flowers swallowed you up in a brilliant landscape.

O'Brien had been to the restaurant often, it being the choice of many out of town clients. Still, the aloofness of the Maitre'd was unchanged. O'Brien's mood fell another notch.

"I'm Mr. O'Brien, I believe my wife is here."

"*Oui, Monsieur*," He gestured toward the lounge area. "*Madame* will be with you *tout de suite*. Let me show you to your table."

O'Brien had observed from his previous visits that the restaurant had tables variously positioned to cater to the desires of the clientele, whether one wanted to be seen or not to be seen, to see or not to see. As they headed toward the rear, on the left were four dark-suited men engaged in animated conversation. One pointed with a lamb chop to make a point. An elegant older couple sat secluded in a banquet, impervious to the men and everything but themselves. Near the back, the Maitre'd stopped at a table below a magnificent mural of the French seaside. It was one of the most visible tables in the restaurant. O'Brien knew the Maitre'd had a reputation for placing a beautiful woman as a centerpiece. Helen had struck him as deserving of this honor.

"*Bon appétit, Monsieur*, I'm sure *Madame* will be here shortly."

Just as the man turned away, Helen emerged at the front of the room. She walked erect, her round head held high — the top of the upside down exclamation point described by her body. She moved slowly, gracefully toward him. The four men stopped talking, the one lowered his lamb chop. This was a familiar scene to O'Brien, one he had relished in the early days of the marriage. Nothing pleased Helen more than to stop a room. There would be other excursions taken before the night was over. She sat down and through a tight smile whispered, "How could you do this? Make me wait an hour?"

"There are worse places to wait."

"You're never late for that God-damned agency."

"It provides you with a pretty great lifestyle. He took a breath, lowered his voice. "Look, we're in this place because it was your idea, so let's enjoy it."

"Will you? Or, are you bored with eating in these fancy spots?"

"Right, like the group of men down there. That's what it's like when I go to these restaurants."

"You expect me to believe that? What a laugh. I know what goes on on Madison Avenue, about all the women in the business today. Everyone we know says you hardly pay attention to me."

Everyone meant Karen Miles, Helen's best — only — friend. But, O'Brien didn't want to take the bait. "Can we call a truce, just for dinner? Here comes the captain, let's order."

O'Brien's mind drifted while the captain went through an elaborate recitation of the offerings not listed on the menu. He found himself envying another couple at a nearby table, they were laughing, holding hands. And that elderly couple had seemed to be in love.

"*Monsieur*?"

"Yes, I'll have the roast veal and a salad to start."

"How pedestrian," said Helen before the captain left.

O'Brien avoided the insult. "How's Tommy?" he asked instead, immediately regretting the wide opening he'd given her.

She relished the opportunity, fought back a smile. "Tommy's fine. You wouldn't have to ask if you were home more often." She leaned back, satisfied.

O'Brien moved in, livid. "Look, we've been through all this. I'm the creative director of a big agency. It's demanding."

"Which means if I say your son needs a father, I'm being demanding and I shouldn't be, right?"

"I know Tommy needs me, and you know I love him." He placed both hands on the edge of the table.

"I didn't say you didn't love him. My point is, that's not enough. He needs you to be there."

She had won the round. "Fine, once again, you've made me feel guilty about the amount of time I spend with Tommy." He signalled a passing waiter. "I'd like a martini, please, on the rocks ... make it with Tanqueray gin ... and add some onions."

"*Oui, Monsieur*, a Tanqueray gibson." He sped off.

"You don't drink martinis. You hardly drink at all. What's this? I guess being with me for an evening makes you need to drink."

"It's my birthday, remember? I'm celebrating."

"Well, in that case ..." She reached into her purse, took out a small pale blue box, Tiffany. She handed it to him. "Hope you like them."

He opened the box. Inside were silver cuff links, simple, with his initials in script, the kind the chairman wore, the only man at the agency O'Brien could think of who wore French cuffs. Most of the young creative types wouldn't even recognize a cuff link if they found one lying in the street. "They're beautiful," he said, knowing he would never wear them. The cuff links were part of a long term scheme of Helen's to turn him into the banker her father was, if only in dress.

"I'm glad you like them. I think you should be more formal in your dress ... for someone with a big job like yours, someone who wants to be president of the agency some day. The way you dress for work, I think the neighbors wonder if you really are an executive."

It was just one more example of her ignorance of the way the agency business worked. Hopeless. He pointed at his empty martini glass to the passing waiter, who nodded. She didn't understand that casual dress at the agency was as much a uniform to him as the black, pin-striped suit, cuff links, white shirt and winged tip shoes were to her banker father. Helen wanted his clothes to be a signal to the neighborhood of her high standing. He considered going into it, but was saved by the waiter.

"Escargots, *Madame*?"

Helen, too, was distracted from their match. "Oh, smell them, smell the garlic."

Impulsively, O'Brien resolved to do his part to make the rest of the dinner a success. The restaurant certainly did its part. Helen even broke her no-dessert rule and agreed to a raspberry souffle. The delay in bringing this delicacy afforded her a last opportunity to walk the room. He watched her go, toyed with the cuff links.

One thing Helen had been right about was his goal of being agency president. But she had no idea how strong his emotions were. His intensity at work was seen by his associates as part of his attention to detail, his perfectionism. While he cared about every ad, he saw them increasingly as a means to an end, the end being the vacant corner office on the executive floor, the office left open by the early retirement of the past president. Only the chairman knew of O'Brien's obsession with the presidency. The chairman kept his options open, but it was clear to O'Brien from their conversations that he had a clear shot at the job if he just kept the quality of the agency's creative work at the star level it had attained under his guidance.

And now his entire career could be derailed by the Global mess. Instead of becoming president he could ... it was hard to believe ... but he could be in trouble or worse if the largest account were lost.

"Are you drunk? You look like you're in a haze." She fished in her purse. "Here's the garage receipt, the car's across the street. I'll wait here. It's raining hard. I don't want to ruin my hair."

He was grateful to get away. Even into a hard rain. He dashed across the street, dodged the water-filled pot holes, was splashed by a cab zooming by. He had trouble reading the wet parking ticket, looked up and down the street. There was no garage in sight. He went into the St. Regis hotel, found a bellhop, learned the garage was back across the street, next to La Côte Basque. He was drenched when he got to the garage. How could she be so careless, so inconsiderate? Once inside the car, he slammed his fist against the dashboard. He resolved to himself that he wouldn't delay any longer. It was time to act.

. . .

The Island of San Sebastian

Murphy reached under the table to be sure his briefcase was there. He scanned the room, scrunched himself further to the back of the booth in an attempt to become inconspicuous. It was a tough assignment. The bar was jammed with islanders, with a sprinkling of American honeymooners. In his dark, wrinkled Paul Stuart suit, white button-downed shirt and blue and red tie, he couldn't have looked more out of place.

Murphy's mood was out of synch with the rest of the room. Loud conversation and laughter reverberated against the Calypso music coming from the band on the veranda nearest the beach. He looked toward the door, then at his watch. Why did the Minister insist that they meet at this crowded, public place?

Murphy looked up to see the waitress at his table. "*Un otro Cuba libre, Conchita, por favor.* And get these honeymooners out of here. Why aren't they in their beds where they belong?"

"Because they were shacked up for five years before they got hooked, *Señor.*"

"Well, it pisses me off."

"Maybe the Minister will bring you a surprise to make you happy, a honeymoon special." She giggled as she left.

Shit, did everybody in San Sebastian know what was going on? If they knew about the women, what else did they know? And, today, in the stairwell, what was that remark from Clay Walker about being late for his bookie?

He looked over at the door again, took a long drink from his glass. There wasn't much good about his gambling lately. He was on a long losing streak. He still couldn't get over his loss on the Knick game two nights before. They had always gone into the tank on their third away game in a row. And here they'd actually won the game outright. It had to be Reilly, he had the team ready, even on the road. He would have to avoid going against the Knicks for a while.

He took a sheet of paper from his pocket and wrote down some numbers. He did the numbers a second time to be sure. They came out the same. He was twenty-two thousand in the hole. This trip couldn't have come at a more opportune time. It wasn't smart to get behind in his payments to the boys in New York.

Where was the bastard, anyhow? He made up his mind he was going to put his foot down with the Minister. No more public meetings in bars like this. He was thinking about going to the men's room when the Minister arrived amid loud fanfare from the natives. Everybody on the island seemed to know him. That wasn't good either. The Minister shook a line of hands on his way to the booth.

"Pardon me, *Señor*, have you seen a *Señor* Murphy, an American, dark suit, red hair, sort of a horny little guy?"

"Cut the bullshit, Ramon. Where the fuck you been anyway?"

"Such language. You will offend the virgin ears of Regina." A native girl came up next to the Minister. "Regina, meet *Señor* Murphy. *Señor* Murphy, meet Regina. Regina is studying to be a model, perhaps a television actress, maybe be in commercials, go to New York, meet all the bigshots on Madison Avenue." He looked over and smiled, put his arm around her and drew her toward him. "I said, you gotta meet *Señor* Murphy. He can arrange such things. I think you two should have a long conversation on such matters. But, later. Regina, leave us alone for a while. Take a walk on the beach. Show *Señor* Murphy how nice you walk. Regina has had training."

The girl slid out of the booth, bending over in an exaggerated fashion toward Murphy to show off her breasts. She walked slowly toward the door, swaying back and forth in time with the Calypso beat. A handful of men at the bar watched her leave, then stared at Murphy and the Minister.

"I don't like meeting here in public, Ramon. You can't trust these people."

"Who cares? What do they know? Who they gonna talk to? The C.I.A.? Forget it. You Madison Avenue guys are too uptight. Relax, for Christ's sake. Now, let's get down to business. It's late. Then, you can spend the rest of the night casting the girl for the next commercial."

"It doesn't make good business sense to keep meeting here, Ramon."

"Can we get started, please?" He leaned across the table toward Murphy. Murphy could smell the onions on his breath. "I've got big news for you. The numbers are changing, everything's going up. Your payment is going up and my payment is going up. Call it inflation."

"What the hell are you talking about?"

"The good news is the advertising budget is now up to fifteen million bucks. That should make you an even bigger hero at the agency." He looked around the room. "And, we're raising my little consultancy fee from six-hundred-fifty thousand to seven-hundred and fifty." He put up both hands in front of him. "Before you get your balls in an uproar you should be happy to know that your kickback is going from two-twenty-five to two-hundred-and-fifty thousand."

"I like the way you call your payment a consultancy fee and mine a kickback. When was the last time you did any consulting for us? What a joke."

"Call it what you want." The Minister smiled and slipped a pack of Camels from his jacket pocket, offered one to Murphy, then withdrew it. "I forgot, you just like gambling, booze and broads." He lit up, took a deep drag, watched the smoke circle upward. "Let's remember, Murphy, this is a good deal for everybody. The agency gets to do some fancy commercials at a nice profit, and we both get to enjoy a better life style. It's the American way. Now, where's your case?"

The ritual had become a familiar one to Murphy. He was proud that it had been his idea that they buy two identical briefcases. When they met, Murphy would bring an empty one and the Minister would exchange it for the one with the money. Now Murphy slid his case from under his legs and passed it under the table to the Minister, who passed the second case back.

The Minister stood. "*Adiós, Amigo.* Have a good time tonight with your casting session."

Regina passed the Minister as he headed for the bar. "Drinks for everyone," he shouted, waving his arms over his head, pointing to the bartender. "Pedro, what time is it? Isn't it time for some real music?"

The bartender looked at his watch, reached under the bar. The circular bar began to transform. Floor-to-ceiling mirrors interspersed about the edge of the room rotated back and forth. Flashing light waves generated from above the center of the bar blinked and bounced against the moving panes of glass. The gentle music of the group on the veranda was overwhelmed by harsher metal sounds. The effect was one of visual and aural disorientation.

Murphy couldn't hear. He took the girl in one arm, the briefcase in the other. He guided her to the exit, lagging slightly behind, his eyes riveted to the movement of her torso.

• • •

DAY 29

P.J.'s Bar & Grille, New York City

Clay Walker sat at his favorite corner booth at P.J.'s, an agency hangout halfway between the office and Grand Central. The corner provided him with a view of the entire room and was adjacent to the hallway to the rest rooms, allowing him to converse with any of his associates headed that way.

Clay shifted back and forth on the wooden seat, an action necessitated by some unremoved shrapnel fragments. If he remained static, the pieces began to irritate, not a sharp pain, but a dull soreness. He could hear the thunderstorm outside. Cold and rain made his situation worse. It was unusually chilly for May 15th in New York. The doctors said that the pieces were too small to be excised and the problem would alleviate itself over time. That had been in Viet Nam twenty-five years earlier. Doctors he had consulted since made the same conclusion.

"Clay, I hear you've added another account. The cranberry folks." This, from a fellow senior vice president.

"It's true, Jack. And they tell me there are a lot more cranberries than the country needs."

"Well, tell them to double their advertising budget."

"I will, you can be sure."

Now he shifted in his seat to get a clear line of sight to the bartender. Years ago, Clay and the bartender had worked out a signal system patterned after the way catchers and pitchers communicated in baseball. The bartender would show one finger, indicating a single shot. Clay would either approve or shake his head no. If his response was negative the bartender would change the signal to two fingers, indicating a double. They would proceed until Clay agreed, and the waitress would deliver the drink. The system prevented others from knowing exactly how much Clay was drinking.

He drank Cutty Sark, which due to its light color, didn't look strong in double, or even triple doses. Clay had christened the bartender Yogi Berra in honor of his signal calling skills. The regulars at P.J.'s knew the bartender as Yogi, but were ignorant of the significance of the name.

A dark suit obstructed his view of Yogi. "What train are you planning on, Clay?"

"I have no immediate plan as of now, Frank, you'll have to go it on your own."

The advertising world had turned upside down. Not that many years before, two and three martini lunches were routine. Now, no one drank at lunch, hardly went out to lunch. Then, no one talked about a problem, although Clay knew more marines that had died from swollen livers than from enemy bullets. Now, while few drank at all, there were posters about alcohol abuse all over the agency. Personally, he couldn't figure what was wrong with a couple of pops after a hard day's work. After all, he never drank during the day. And he found the alcohol aided his persuasive powers when he pursued his various ladies.

The busy bartender was signaling with one finger. Clay nodded his agreement. Behind Yogi, Clay could see Dennis O'Brien emerging as he headed toward Clay's booth.

"Dennis, how goes it? Up to your ass in alligators as usual? What's this I hear about Global?"

The girl arrived with Clay's drink. "Would you like a beer, Mr. O'Brien?"

"I would, a Bud Lite will do the trick, Estelle." He waited until the girl had left. "What do you know about Global?"

Clay held his hands up like an orator. "Three may keep a secret if two of them are dead."

"Shakespeare?"

"No, Ben Franklin."

"Anyway, no one's supposed to know."

"So, I'm right. Something is up. What's the scoop, fellow jarhead? I'm cleared for top secret, as you know." He grinned at O'Brien.

"It's still murky. Yesterday, Murphy got this cryptic note out of the blue, putting us on notice."

"I thought the account was all sweetness and light."

"It is, or was. What happened today is Brad talked to their chairman, Haps Corwin, a guy who's been our friend."

"And?"

"It's true, we are on notice, but Corwin said not to worry. It seems their new president, Bill Swenson, convinced the board that all suppliers should be reevaluated, and we're one of the suppliers, to use Swenson's term. Corwin told Brad that the airline is losing ten million a month and Swenson was brought in to fix it."

"I don't know much about him, except the *Wall Street Journal* paints him as a boy genius. He was a super star at Citibank. And, a fucking fly boy, by the way. One of those air force guys who dropped bombs five miles from the line while we were getting our asses kicked by the gooks." Clay sipped his drink.

"I know his history. He's something to contend with. Brad came back from his meeting and said to treat this like a five alarmer."

"Just what you need, another crisis. Do you ever get any sleep?"

"Hey, you're the one who looks like he was out all night. What's the bump on your forehead? You're the only person I know who spends half his time chasing old girlfriends. Why don't you go home once in a while?"

"How do you think I got this bump? Cathy got me with the miniature souvenir Yankee bat I bought Andy. At least my old girlfriends are happy to see me ... Usually."

"With all your clients I don't know how you handle it. Maybe you're one of the reasons Brad is sending us to Outward Bound."

"What the hell are you talking about?"

"After the Global thirty days are over, he's sending all the senior executives, two at a time, to a two-week Outward Bound program outside of Atlanta. Supposed to toughen us up, rekindle our spirits, that sort of thing."

"No way, José. This is one gyrene who is not going camping. I had my fill of the outdoor life courtesy of the U.S. morons. My ass still hurts from all the metal the V.C.'s put in it." Clay shifted in his seat and peered toward the bar, looking for Yogi.

"I don't relish climbing into a sleeping bag again either. But I heard Brad talk about it and he's serious."

"If that's the case, I'm requesting you as my partner, Dennis. But, I'm starting right now to think of ways to squelch this madness in the bud."

"I wish you all the luck in the world." O'Brien got up. "I have to go back to the office, work on the plan for saving Global."

Clay reached into his pocket and came up empty. "Say, Dennis, do you have a quarter handy?"

"Which is it this time? The girl from Chappaqua or the one from Ho-Ho-Kus."

"I haven't decided." He watched O'Brien leave, called after him. "Did I ever tell you about the Irish girl from Nodine Hill in Yonkers?"

O'Brien kept going, shaking his head. He took the problem list from his coat pocket, but his mind was on how he would handle his divorce. What a time to have this to deal with. It was incredible to him that Helen already had a lawyer, as if the man was in the wings, waiting for his cue. Had she been planning this all along? And, what had his lawyer said in their first conversation? ... that O'Brien would have to spend a good deal of time working with him on an affidavit and some other papers. And, Helen had hired one of the roughest divorce lawyers in the country. That he should be prepared for a long and expensive fight.

. . .

San Sebastian

The strange surroundings and his hangover combined to confuse Murphy. The crashing sound of the ocean on the beach outside gradually brought him back to reality. Then, he saw the girl next to him. Carefully, he rolled over, avoided waking her. His head hurt and the back of his tongue was sore. He carried the telephone as far from the bed as possible to a sofa, sat and dialed.

"Hi, Maureen, it's me, how's everything?" He looked at the girl. She looked ravishing in the dim light. She seemed to be sound asleep. "That's too bad, did you take him to the doctor?"

The girl opened one eye, looked over at Murphy.

"It's hard to say, I've got a whole day of meetings here."

The girl sat up in bed, yawned, smiled across at Murphy. The sheet fell away, exposing her perfect breasts.

"Well, at least this account seems to be in good shape. The Minister and I get along well together."

Lackadaisically, the girl walked around the room, peered out the window at the beach. She glanced at Murphy's attaché case, slightly ajar on the table by the sofa.

"Has there been anything in the paper about the Global account?"

The girl leaned over, peeked into the briefcase, jumped back in surprise, slowly breathing, "*Caramba.*"

"Well, that's good. It's hard enough as it is. We don't need any publicity. Every agency in town would kill for the Global business." Murphy waved his hands, signaling the girl away from his case.

The girl took a packet from the case and removed the surrounding band. She threw the money into the air. The new bills flew about the room, spinning and fluttering to the floor.

Murphy held his hand over the phone, gestured toward the girl. He whispered, "Regina, no. Stop it." To the phone he said, "I'm not sure when I'll get back to New York. I'll probably have to go straight to the office because of Global."

The girl unwrapped two packs of bills. She climbed onto the bed and began to jump up and down. Her breasts bounced as she waved her arms, tossing the crisp money toward the ceiling with both hands. The new bills descended like little paper helicopters, covering the bed in green.

Murphy held the phone between his neck and his shoulder. He walked toward the girl, tripped on the phone line. The girl dodged him, grabbed several additional packets. She ran around the room laughing, throwing the bills in every direction.

"Look, Maureen, I've got to get going. I'm running late for my meeting with the Minister. Give my love to the kids, tell them I'll see them soon." He tried to trip the girl as she went by, but missed. "I love you too, dear." He dropped the phone, tackled the girl. They fell across the bed into a pile of cash.

The girl giggled, pulled Murphy toward her. "*Señor* Murphy, the native men have nothing on you." She rolled over on top of him.

Murphy forgot about his aching head, was only vaguely aware of the nearby surf. His last thought was that the Minister would have to wait for him this time.

. . .

The girl watched as Murphy headed down the path toward the main building of the resort. She sat on the bed, wondering how she would spend the money Murphy had given her from the piles she had neatly rearranged for him. She knelt down by the bed and peered under it, hoping that a bill or two might have drifted there. Only the tiny tape recorder was visible. She picked up the machine and placed it in her carry-all. She got up, dialed the phone.

"Ramon, I have the tape. We had a good time, a noisy one. You'll like it. I'll meet you at five at the usual place."

• • •

DAY 28

Burns & Cody

"Go on in, Sandy. He should be back any minute. Make yourself at home."

"Thanks, Evelyn." Sandy checked her watch. She was early for her meeting with O'Brien. He'd said something about the Global account when he called. It was an account that O'Brien knew well, but one that she had not worked on during her nine years at the agency.

She felt comfortable in O'Brien's office even though she had rarely been in it. Any place that was filled with art made her happy. Except for the hammock, the office looked like a creative director's office. Paintings and prints covered the walls. Memorabilia, photos and personal items were spread across his desk and the tables. Advertising in every stage of finish, from raw ideas to completed proofs, was spread about the room. A shelf in the corner held an impressive array of creative awards that O'Brien had won. The awards were an important contributor to

O'Brien's creative reputation, not just within the agency, but throughout the industry. Directly above his desk was the framed front page of *Adweek* announcing the agency's selection as Agency of the Year for 1994.

Another corner of the office displayed a montage of personal pictures, his friends and his family, going back to his youth. There was even a baby picture, left over from the time he had issued a catalogue of the entire creative department, challenging members to identify the grown-ups from their earlier incarnations. It had been easy, Sandy remembered, to pick O'Brien's baby picture. Even then he had those intelligent eyes, somehow an expression of confidence.

Sandy surveyed the wall. There was a picture of him in a cassock and surplice, as an altar boy outside of the Christ the King Church. There was O'Brien and a group of teenage friends in front of a school. "Hastings High School" was clearly legible on the front of the building. Sandy recalled she and her husband, once on a trip to the Adirondacks to go rafting, going through the little Hudson River town, Hastings on Hudson, a hilly community just north of New York City.

Growing older and muscular, there was O'Brien in his M.I.T. wrestling uniform. There were several Marines Corps pictures, a group of lieutenants at what appeared to be an officers' graduation ceremony, one of him standing before a row of giant mortars, another of a half dozen Marines in a Viet Nam village. There were many shots of his son and an equal number of their miniature poodle. Both the boy and the dog were familiar to agency people from their frequent visits to O'Brien's office. Several pictures showed O'Brien and his son engaged in some activity: biking, sledding, ball playing. The animal was usually in hot pursuit of one of them. Standing back from the display it occurred to Sandy that in every photo O'Brien was either smiling or laughing. He hadn't changed much in appearance or demeanor over the years.

"See anyone you recognize?" O'Brien entered the room in a rush, his arms full of video tapes. "Those pictures remind me of happy times. They help me when clients become unreasonable, like Global all of a sudden." He pointed toward a chair. "Here, grab a seat and let me tell you what this is all about."

Sandy took the seat offered, but found it too deep, considering the short skirt she wore. She elected to sit on the front edge of the chair, pulling her dress forward, leaning toward O'Brien.

He studied her for a second, looked only briefly at the line where her shapely legs and her skirt met. She was known around the agency as a Meg Ryan look alike. It was true, she had all-American looks, plus an enthusiasm that enhanced her prettiness.

She began talking. "You said this was about Global."

"Yes, I want you to supervise the creative teams and also to work with me as part of an extra team."

"That sounds great, but I don't know anything about the account."

"That could be a plus. You bring a totally fresh viewpoint. And you're our senior art director, so it's about time you got involved with our biggest account."

"There isn't much time."

"True, but I've got six writer-art director teams assigned, not counting the two of us, so you'll have a lot of help. Most of the people have airline experience, if not Global."

"How do I get up to speed?"

"First, with these tapes. Five years of advertising, good and bad. Mostly good."

"And, the latest work?"

"You know that an airline runs a bunch of splinter campaigns, against business flyers, for example, or vacationers, even seasonal efforts of different kinds. In order to tie all of these together we've always had an umbrella campaign, something to unify all the other work."

"Like the 'Global Pride' campaign."

"Correct, an idea that we sold against my better judgment. Haps Corwin over at Global loved it. But, it's loaded with ... "

"Clichés."

"You hit it. Corwin thought the campaign would make employees proud to be part of the airline. But, showing airline personnel is the oldest trick in advertising. Boring. But, the real danger was using the word 'pride' with Global, an airline with an average reputation. The phrase 'Global Pride' was risky from the start. It implies that there's something to be proud of. More important, it says there is nothing to be unproud of."

"The minute you make a mistake the line backfires."

"Right, and they made plenty of mistakes, even before the crash in San Antonio."

"Is that when the campaign was pulled?"

"Typically, an airline stops advertising for a few weeks after a crash. They've all had their share. People tend to forget after a while. But, in our case, because of all the financial problems at the airline, they decided not to take up the campaign again. We've been off the air for two months."

O'Brien's secretary entered the office. "I'm sorry to interrupt, but your wife says it's important."

"Not now, Evelyn. Please tell her I'll call her back." He looked at Sandy, tried to pick up the thread of conversation.

"If they walked away from the advertising I assume we've been working on a replacement campaign."

"The only thing we have so far is a strategy statement. There's a copy of it in that pile of reference material."

"What's the gist of it?"

"It's based on the one unique aspect about Global, geographical coverage. They fly to more cities in more countries than any airline."

"And flyers like bigness?"

"It works two ways, it makes them think of Global as a possible alternative more often and it makes them feel more comfortable."

"Meaning safe?"

"Safe without ever saying it."

"What's the next step? What should I do?"

"I want you to familiarize yourself with the past work, also talk to the creative teams to find out where they stand. You know most of them, I'm sure. How long have you been at the agency now?"

"It's nine years. I came here directly from Pratt."

"A Pratt brat, I knew that." He stood up and walked to his desk. "The other thing is the music. Normally, for the airline, I wouldn't get the music people involved until we had a theme line and a clear idea of what the campaign looked like, complete with a bunch of storyboards, but in this case ... "

"There's no time." She smiled at him.

He laughed. "I was thinking this morning, it's 28 days now. Anyway, I've got five music houses, two here, two in L.A., and one in Nashville. We'll be making music on the run, blending it in with what we end up with as the campaign, adjusting as we go." He winced. "We'll be on the leading edge of the business."

"An expensive edge."

"The most ever spent on a speculative pitch. I told the chairman it could run to two million before we're finished and if we lose we'll have to eat it."

"What did he say about that?"

"He said for a one-hundred million dollar account you do whatever it takes to keep the business because the alternative is unacceptable. If we don't win, a lot of people here are going to be gone and there won't be any bonuses for the rest of us for quite a while."

"I wasn't planning on going anywhere during the next month."

"Good, none of us are. So, let's go. Let me know when you need me for anything."

"Great, I will." Sandy picked up the piles of tapes and correspondence.

"You look like a high school student after the first day of school."

She smiled at him, nodded to Evelyn as she passed, headed down the hallway past her own office to an inside room which the department used for coffee breaks and informal meetings. The room contained a large table, six chairs, a refrigerator, sink, some cupboards and an assortment of kitchen utensils. The space reminded her of the small kitchen in her home in Milwaukee.

She took a Coke from the refrigerator, sat down, let out a deep breath. The meeting with O'Brien was unique. With little fanfare she'd been given the biggest assignment of her career, one that would have total visibility around the agency. If the agency kept the business there was no telling what it might mean for her career. There had been rumors that O'Brien had a good shot at the job of president, an open position since the last agency president's early retirement for health reasons. If O'Brien moved up, the job of creative director would be open. She had dreamed of the possibility of someday becoming the top creative person in the agency, but never thought it could materialize so soon.

She was pleased at how she had kept her cool during the meeting, acted as if it were just another assignment, though she could barely contain her sense of the excitement ahead.

The idea of working directly with O'Brien as part of a creative team was exciting in itself. She liked him and knew she would learn from him. He would be thoughtful and supportive when the crunch came. There was something reassuring about the man's confidence. It seemed to flow from him into others, shoring them up when the pressure was on. It was part of his agency reputation. Even his office gave off a feeling of warmth and steadiness, a reflection of him. She could clearly recall many of the photos from the corner display. For a second she wondered why among the hundred or so pictures there was just one of his wife, a dated one of the two of them. She was an attractive woman, but she appeared to be posing.

Suddenly Sandy realized the room she was in made her uncomfortable. It was too much like home. She had worked hard at forgetting about Milwaukee and her family. But this room broke through her shield, bringing back unwanted memories. The room reminded her of her mother, a person she despised, a weak woman who was a servant to the needs of her father and her four brothers. When she thought along these lines, the day she'd come home early from school was part of it. She could still hear the strange sounds from her parents bedroom, sounds that had drawn her upstairs to hear better, the grunting of her father and the brevity of the encounter. Her father had said, "It's too bad you never enjoyed this." To her mother it was just another chore to be done, like a sink full of dirty dishes.

Her mother, in denying her own needs, didn't acknowledge those of the other female member of the group. Those men, a butcher and his four soon-to-be butcher sons, practicing their three B's: beer, bratwurst and bowling. It was ludicrous if it hadn't been so sad. Only her art had saved her, helped her escape.

She looked at the wall clock. It was 7:00 pm. She had work to do. She was at the crux of a crises that would have historic impact on the agency. It would either be a great triumph or a calamity. Her role would be pivotal.

• • •

DAY 27

Global Airlines, New York City

From the Global board room on the 53rd floor Fran Irwin enjoyed the view of Rockefeller Center. It was a perfect spring day, ideal for the sightseers that swarmed below. She could see a bus unloading a group of Japanese tourists, each hitting the pavement, camera ready. She avoided the conversation of Maynard Baxter and Jack Kreeger behind her.

"Why do you think Mr. Swenson wants to talk to us, Maynard?"

"He's the president of the airline, Jack, why wouldn't he want to meet with us?"

"I'm not used to meeting with people at his level. When I was in sales I never met the president."

"Well, Jack, you're not in sales now."

"Besides, I've already met with Mr. Swenson a couple of times. He interviewed me before I became advertising director."

"It shows that he takes an interest in what's going on. He's living up to his reputation as a man of action. Right, Fran?"

"What? ... Sorry, I wasn't listening."

"We were talking about Swenson."

"I hope it was good." They halted as Swenson walked into the room. "Good morning, I'm Bill Swenson." He shook hands with each of them.

To Fran he couldn't have been more imposing if he had entered the room from the window ledge and wore a cape. She was surprised how much more handsome he was in person. Perhaps it was his outgoing demeanor, the evident energy of the man, that enhanced his looks. Also, he was taller than she'd expected, at least six foot two or three.

"I wanted to meet with you today as the first of a series of regular get-togethers I'm planning to have with senior managers like yourselves. As president, you tend to get a lot of written reports, which is fine, except the reports don't always give you an accurate picture. These meetings will provide us with the opportunity to discuss issues in a frank manner. It will also allow me to update you on what I've been doing. I hope this will keep the rumors down, rumors often being the product of misinformation or ignorance."

Fran detected a trace of Texas accent. She had read everything she could find about him. She knew he had left Texas at an early age to go to school in the east and had never returned.

"The board of Global has asked me to take a stronger role in the day-to-day operations of the airline. That will now include the areas of responsibility represented here: advertising, media and sales promotion. Jack Kreeger and I have already spent some time together. You may have heard that we have put Burns & Cody on thirty days notice. It's part of my belief that no supplier should ever assume it has a cozy relationship with the airline. It's been my experience that companies, and people as well, need constant goads and incentives to bring out their very best performance. And the best is what we seek."

Fran could see why people were saying that Swenson was going to have a dramatic impact on the airline. Perhaps this was the answer to her own dilemma.

"Now, let's start on this side of the table." He pointed at Fran's boss. She wondered if Baxter looked as ugly to Swenson as he appeared to her. Baxter's face today was more tomato-like than usual: red, round and blotchy. His tiny eyes peered out at Swenson.

"My name is Maynard Baxter. I'm vice president of media and sales promotion. I've been with the airline for ten years. Before that I worked for Burns & Cody and for NBC."

"You have a big responsibility here. I believe the advertising budget is over one-hundred million and the sales promotion budget is about half of that."

"That's correct."

"Burns & Cody is by far the biggest supplier, but there must be other sources, particularly in sales promotion."

"Yes, that's true. Fran Irwin, here, runs all of our sales promotion activities. She can tell you more about that area."

Swenson looked at Fran, "Tell me a little about your background, Fran."

"I started at Global right out of Hofstra about fifteen years ago, started as the most junior assistant in the sales promotion department. And, you're right, we have many suppliers of sales promotion materials, over a dozen in fact, specialists in the different forms of the business."

"That's interesting. We will want to examine these suppliers, too. For the time being, give me a complete list of them, along with their dollar volumes and the lengths of time of their relationships with the airline. Also, brief evaluations of them and a ranking of them from best to worst."

Swenson pointed at Kreeger, but looked at Maynard and Fran. "You've met Jack Kreeger, our new advertising vice president. Jack was transferred out of sales just a few weeks ago, right Jack?"

Kreeger looked at Swenson's feet. "I've been with the airline for twelve years, all in sales, in different parts of the country. I've moved around a lot."

Fran tried not to stare at Kreeger's ears. Besides being disproportionately large for his head, they stood out at an angle. This was particularly noticeable when he faced someone directly. Fran found it awkward to look at him.

"The letter to Burns & Cody putting them on notice did go out?"

"Just like you told me, it went out three days ago."

"Has there been any reaction?"

"They were very surprised and upset. Malachy Murphy, who runs the account for them, said it was completely unfair."

"Did he?"

"He said that they wanted to meet you, that you haven't been to the agency. They would like to give you an orientation session."

"That's fine with me. We'll arrange to do that soon." He paused. "Now, in the case of the agency, we expect them to make a presentation in a month. At that time a vote will be taken to decide whether or not to retain them. There are six voters, the four people in this room plus Mr. Corwin, of course, and also Ted Crowther, the marketing director. If the vote is tied, there will be a member of the board of directors present who will cast the deciding vote."

Baxter raised his hand, "Do you intend to look at other agencies?"

"We'll see. I want you, Jack, to put together a file on the top five agencies that don't have an airline account. We may want to ask one or two of them to make a presentation as a basis of comparison. Any other questions?" Swenson looked at each of them. "Good. I'd like to have these meetings twice a month." He started toward the door. "Jack, please come with me. I want to talk about the other agencies for a minute."

Baxter watched them leave, turned to Fran. "Well, Fran, an interesting development. Obviously, a man of action. A true West Pointer. I like his military demeanor, don't you?"

"What are you driving at?"

"He strikes me as someone who thrives on change. A smart person would watch him closely."

"I'm sure you will. And I'm sure he'll be watching us."

"I can't imagine what you mean by that, Fran. As for us, he won't be able to watch too closely since we'll be gone most of the month. In fact, we leave for the islands on Friday, I believe." He smiled, showing his uneven teeth, and patted her on the shoulder. Fran cringed.

They walked to the elevators. The meeting had convinced Fran that Swenson was going to be involved. The question was: How far would he delve into their activities? How much would he uncover? On the one hand it gave her hope. On the other, it terrified her.

. . .

P.J.'s

O'Brien looked across at his friend. "Fancy red suspenders. I've never thought of you as clothes conscious."

"Through tattered clothes small vices do appear; Robes and furred gowns hide all."

"Ben Franklin?"

Clay shook his head in satisfaction. "Shakespeare, King Lear. But, I'm not trying to make a fashion statement. Between you and me, my trousers have been feeling a little tight lately. It's was painful to sit down. If I wore my trousers loose I'd have to keep pulling them up. The suspenders were the answer to the problem. Form follows function."

"Very creative. But, let me ask you something. Is it true what I hear about Chicago?"

"I don't know, what did you hear?"

"I heard you pulled the top of the client's bathing suit down and tried to kiss her."

"That's consistent with the other reports I've gotten." Clay tried to make out Yogi Berra's signal, but it was blocked by a customer at the bar.

"Well, what happened? Is it true?"

"Damned if I know. I was pretty shot by that point."

O'Brien held his hands to his head. "You mean you don't know what happened?"

"I remember a bunch of us from the agency and a few clients deciding to take a swim after dinner. People sort of disappeared to find something to wear in the pool. I just got rid of my suit and went in in my skivvies. She showed up in the water and was kind of playful. I guess I took her up on her invitation. You should see those knockers. Hall of Fame, believe me."

"But, then?"

"I guess she didn't want her associates to see the real her, a humanoid."

"What do you mean?"

"You don't know this client. Miss MBA. I think she overdosed on the Dale Carnegie course. Miss Success. Except she's always in a mini skirt, or a split dress, or a tight blouse. At night, it's worse, or better, depending on your point of view. So she wants to be treated like a man, but she acts like a woman. Well, she went too far in the pool as far as I'm concerned."

Open-mouthed, O'Brien listened. "So, it's really her fault?"

Clay held his hands up and raised his voice in imitation of a woman. "C'mon Clay. I'll race you to the end of the pool." Then, when I got ahead of her, she grabbed my leg and we bumped into each other. That was pretty playful, too. So I grabbed her knockers. Too bad the others were around, it could have been an interesting aquatic experience."

"You're too much. Even for you, this is a good one. With a client, none the less. I'm worried about you."

The waitress brought Clay a single Cutty Sark. "Yogi couldn't read your sign," was her only comment, like a pitching coach admonishing the pitcher. Clay took the drink and turned back to O'Brien.

"Look, Dennis, you are always worried about me. Maybe you should worry about yourself."

O'Brien put his beer down. As close as they were, his friend rarely went into his personal life.

Clay went on. "We're both unhappily married. We both work our asses off. In my case I take out my frustrations in booze and a little female companionship. I don't know what you do. Probably suffer. Maybe I'm heading for rehab, maybe you're heading for the psycho ward. Think about that. One thing I know, I'm having more fun. It's at least exciting ... sometimes a little too exciting. Why don't you try it? I think you've got the burning ones for Sandy. And as far as I can tell she's hot for you, but doesn't realize it. After all, she's been widowed for two years, something's got to give. Think about that, too."

O'Brien slowly poured his beer into his glass, remained silent.

"Well?"

"Look, you've hit a sensitive note. I wasn't going to say anything to anyone, but I'm sure it will get out somehow. Besides, I know I can trust you." He drank some of the beer. "I can, can't I?"

Clay leaned toward O'Brien, grabbed his arm. "What is it, you're not sick are you?"

"No, it's Helen and I. You as much as anybody know it hasn't been the greatest marriage."

Clay nodded.

"The other night we went out to dinner, it was my birthday. We sat in this expensive restaurant and argued the whole time."

"Argued about what?"

"Usually we argue about the same things, how all I care about is work, how I'm rarely home, which happens to be the truth.

And that I don't love her, which is her constant complaint, since we don't spend much time, you know ... together."

"I get the picture."

"Well, this time I told her that I didn't love her. I was tired of faking it."

"That must have been some restaurant scene."

"It happened after, in the car on the way home. I told her I wanted a divorce."

Clay took a deep breath, finished his drink, sat silent for a moment. "You know, I hate to say it, but it's been obvious to me for years that you had no marriage."

"For a long time I've known I didn't love her, but I finally realized I don't even like her. It's sad. It's a failure."

"And I know how you don't like to fail ... how did she take it?"

"Like a tiger faced with fire. She was as angry as I've ever seen her. Outraged. But, by the time we got home she was bitter, ready for a fight, saying how she was going to take every penny I had, make me pay the price for what I had done to her, that Tommy would now see my true colors. It was a hell of a scene.

"How do you feel?"

"Lousy ... not about the divorce. I feel relieved about that. It's Tommy. He's only ten, you know. And now he's got this unstable family, "dysfunctional" is the vogue word. I told him nothing would change between us, but we both knew it was a lie."

"It doesn't have to be. Kids are stronger than adults realize. Just work hard at it. This isn't the first divorce in history. Lots of kids have survived, even grown from it. Do you think it's better to stay together unhappily, always arguing? Don't you think that effects kids? You better believe it does. Take him on a trip, a long weekend."

"You seem to know a lot about this stuff."

"I do, my parents split when I was in the eighth grade."

"You're kidding. As long as I've known you, I never heard about it. Are you and your father close?"

"What? That prick. I haven't seen him since I joined the Corps. It's the main reason I joined, to get a ticket away from him."

O'Brien was silent. He stared at his glass.

"Hey, everything I said about staying close to your son holds. My father never tried. Too busy with the booze. I know you will. Your life has been one long string of successes. You make a list of things to do every day, priorities. Just make Tommy priority number one." Clay looked over O'Brien's shoulder, caught Yogi's eye, waited for the two finger signal and nodded. "But, don't look so bleak, this doesn't have to be a negative. For example, are you going to start dating? I could fix you up. Better yet, I wasn't kidding about Sandy. She's damned cute and built like a brick you-know-what. You've got her on Global, I hear. Any ulterior motives?"

"You know me better than that. She was the best choice under the circumstances."

"How did she respond?"

"Eagerly, but I think she's scared. Which is normal, considering her experience and what's on the line."

"Nobody at the agency has worked with Sandy more than I, mostly on small accounts that don't get much management attention. I can tell you she has the body of a gazelle, the heart of a lion and the determination of a bull dog." Clay gulped his drink, pointed at O'Brien. "She'd like your job, you know."

"Really? I never thought about her in those terms. I thought of her as a crackerjack art director. And, anybody would have to be blind not to find her attractive."

"Well, think of her again. Before her husband was killed, marriage was number one in her life, white water rafting was second and the job was third. She's one hell of a painter, too. I know they were talking about having kids and her giving up full time work, doing serious painting with whatever time she had."

"You know her pretty well."

"We've been on some out-of-town accounts, you get to talk a lot."

"So, her husband's death must have been devastating."

"Dennis, that's a gross understatement. They lived for each other. After he died she went into a tailspin. The job saved her, that and the gym."

"The gym?"

"When she's not at the agency she's at the gym, working out all her frustrations. She's in unbelievable shape, there's very little jiggle to that lady."

"You'd notice that." O'Brien had a split second image of Sandy sitting on the edge of the chair in his office, leaning toward him.

"I think that her career, and especially the gym, have become substitutes for her real needs."

"Knowing you, I can imagine what you think those are. I thought you were an English major."

"You don't have to be a psychologist to figure her out. You should ask her for a date."

"I don't think that's the smart thing to do right now."

"Maybe not, but think about it." He smiled at O'Brien. "Just think of the possibilities."

"I should be thinking about the Global account and nothing else for the next month."

"What's the latest there?"

"They've set up a panel of voters for a presentation we have to make. From the make-up of the group there are some agency friends and some unknowns. We haven't met Swenson yet. He's coming to the agency next week."

"Any other agencies involved?"

"Thank God, no. That's the most encouraging sign. I think Swenson's the kind of guy who likes to shake things up."

Another round of drinks arrived. Clay took his from the waitress, spilling some as he raised his glass to his lips.

O'Brien looked at him. "You know, this conversation started over the fact that you attacked a client in the swimming pool and all we've talked about are my problems. You're pretty shifty. I want to ask you something." He pointed his finger at him. "What's going on? You seem to be doing some odd things."

"Let me ask you this first. Are any of my clients in trouble?"

"No, not as far as I know."

"I can assure you, they're not. And as you know I have a shitload of them. So I deserve a little R and R occasionally."

"It seems more than occasional to me."

"I've told you before. When I escaped from the V.C.'s I decided I was going to enjoy each day, one at a time."

"A lot of us were in that war."

"Your war and my war were not the same. You were back in that mortar company a mile from the action and then you were a general's aide, with a roof over your head."

"I took the assignments they gave me." He pointed at him again. "Let me tell you something I've never said. One night at your house Cathy let me read your Silver Star citation. She's proud of it. You should be, too. You saved a lot of Marine lives on that hill that day, half dead in the doing."

Walker's eyes watered. He drank a third of his glass slowly, looking at O'Brien as he did so. "I'll tell you what's not on that citation. That was the third time we were told to take that same hill. Every time we moved to a new location the V.C.'s came back. We didn't have enough Marines to hold it. And each time we took the hill back we had fewer Marines to do it. The last day there were wounded Marines all over the place, so I carried some back down. When I came down with the last one the helicopter was gone. So I took a trail back toward our lines. I got about a quarter mile before I realized the Marine was dead. Corporal Serafino, a good man. I'd known him since Pendleton. The next thing I knew I walked straight into this enemy patrol. They had me cold and I was bleeding pretty badly. I woke up in a prison camp."

"That's a hell of a story."

"The story is that the fucking helicopter should have hung in there."

"Maybe he was worried about being trapped on the ground."

"I'm sure he was. And you can bet he didn't want to miss happy hour. It was getting dark."

"So they're wrong and you're right."

"Like I said, I just want to enjoy my life. Work hard, play hard."

O'Brien looked at the man before him in a new light. Then, in an instant, his brain shifted. "Hey, wait a minute, what about the girl in Chicago?"

"Oh, her. Two dozen roses and a phone call and she's happy. Even laughed about it."

"Roses?"

"Oh, my love is like a red, red rose, that's newly sprung in June."

"Shakespeare?"

"No, Robert Burns."

O'Brien threw up his hands. "You're telling me this woman is appeased?"

"Totally. I've put her on my A list. Maybe you'd like to meet her now that you're becoming a free man." He smiled at O'Brien through the top of his tilted glass.

"You're nuts, you know." O'Brien stood up. "But, I have to go. We just got in some music tapes that I have to hear. I'll see you around. Take care of yourself, will you." He headed through the crowded bar, noticed a couple at the bar, their two heads practically touching. Was the girl Sandy? He walked clear around the bar to see better. It wasn't her. He was surprised by the relief he felt.

. . .

East 83rd Street, New York City

He opened the cab door for her and held the umbrella over her head, carried her large art case through the doorway into the lobby. "No matter what shift I'm on, Sandy, you're either going to that agency or coming from it. For one of the biggest agencies in New York it seems to me there oughta be more workers than you."

"We've got hordes of people, believe me."

"Well, why don't you share the work with them? A beautiful lady like you shouldn't spend all her time working."

"Cut the blarney, Kelly." She straightened his cap for him. "A lot of people at the agency put in long hours."

"You should give them more to do so you can relax a little, have the time to find the right man."

"It'll have to wait. The next few weeks are going to be worse than ever. I'm running the biggest pitch we've ever made. Plus, I've got to keep a hand on my regular accounts."

"There's always something with you. What's the point of making all the money if you never get to spend it? The only relaxation you get is going to the gym and I don't count that as relaxation. By the way, I went up and fed Katmandu. I figured you'd want me to, it's so late." He handed her the case. "Here's your elevator." He doffed his cap.

Sandy tried to wave at him, but her hands were full. The man was a big help to her, always seemed to anticipate her needs, like with the cat. He had become her confidant, someone in the big city she could trust. He had a lot of common sense and he made her laugh, too. Since her husband, Kelly had been her main source of shared communication. Her family had never been any use, and since she came to New York they didn't have even a remote understanding of her life. They had fought her coming to art school in the first place, were against her working in the advertising business, and totally rebelled when she told them she was marrying Sid Stein. That had been the final break. She couldn't find any room for respect after that.

There was no one at the agency she could share her feelings with, much less her ambitions. You couldn't trust them. If you told one person a secret you might as well announce it on the agency intercom. "Hi, everyone, this is Sandy Stein and I just want you to know I'm shooting for the creative director's job, so watch your asses."

The elevator stopped at the top floor and opened into the foyer of her apartment. Immediately, she spied the tail of the cat sticking out from behind the sofa at the far end of the living room. She knew she would have to make amends for being so late. The cat would be cool at first, even removed. Sandy called out several times, "Kat, Mommy's home," before the cat appeared shyly from behind the furniture where she had retreated from the sound of the elevator. Katmandu sat across the room and stared at Sandy, determined not to give in easily.

Sandy looked on in admiration. A live work of art was the only way to think of this animal. Infinite shades of brown were represented, beginning with a deep brown nose, mouth and ears, the texture of which were like velvet. From her nose, continuing on to her cheeks and the top of her head, the dark brown lightened to a beige. Out of this dense furry background two blue eyes gazed. The rich coat was beige, too, except for her paws which were as dark as her nose. The cat's silence and stillness were in contrast to her long bushy tail, white at its beginning, but increasingly brown toward the end. Slowly and rhythmically it swooped back and forth in a wide semi-circular motion.

"Mommy's back, she brought you a treat." The cat cocked her head as Sandy took out a small piece of chicken she had saved from lunch. She crumbled the chicken and spread it on the floor, then took a seat on a chair away from the food, allowing the cat to move in without interference.

Sandy scanned the apartment. It smelled nice and clean. The maid had been there, it was Thursday. She went around the living room, straightening, rearranging. The maid had a penchant for moving objects out of place, sort of a mark to prove that she had been there, had justified her pay.

Sandy stopped at her favorite picture. He stood by his raft, the water swirling behind, the epitome of energy, with a smile and a wave. She had taken the picture on a rafting trip down the

Colorado River, only a few months before the accident in Oregon, the fatal trip she could not take because of another agency crisis. The trip she wished she had gone on, to die with him. How he loved rafting, loved life, loved her. It was already two years and she had thought she couldn't last a day without him.

She took the picture and carried it with her into the bedroom. He was the only man she'd met who understood her. And loved her for it. His background, son of immigrant Jews, raised in Hoboken, was a match for her being the daughter of a poor Polish butcher. Sonya Sokolski, what a moniker. Sandy Sokolski had been an improvement, Sandy Stein better yet. In his case, his mind had allowed him to become a scientist, a teacher. She had used art as her tool, first as an escape from within the family, finally as a means of escape altogether. The day her teacher had told her about the scholarship to Pratt had been the happiest day of her life, her independence day.

She stood by the window and stared down at the East River and the street far below. Only a few boats, tiny, were out at this hour. A single cab cruised the street, a small play toy. The distance and the rain added to the peacefulness of the scene. But, reality down there was not tranquility, anymore than a river's rapids, which looked so smooth and harmless from the top of the gorge.

"Kat, I'm supposed to be heading up the saving of the agency's biggest account. It's a make or break situation. Do you think I'm ready?" The cat, the chicken consumed, sat washing her face. She stopped, stared at Sandy from the floor fifteen feet away. She looked interested, but provided no answer. Slowly, she moved toward the chair. Sandy gently put her hand on her neck. The cat snuggled closer and purred. "It's a lonely world out there, isn't it? You and I have to stick together."

. . .

Bedminster, New Jersey

The car came down the ramp too fast, screeched to a halt at the light. He glanced sheepishly at the cop in the adjoining lane. The cop ignored him.

O'Brien looked at his watch for the fifth time since he'd crossed the George Washington Bridge. Ten forty. Tommy most certainly would be in bed. He recounted to himself the points he wanted to make about the divorce, mostly how the two of them would still be father and son, how they would still remain close.

He sped up the winding road, past the country club, toward the top of the ridge. Half of the houses were dark. From the stonewalled entrance to the long driveway he could make out that the lights were off on his son's side of the house. He turned the headlights off on the car, used the glow from the house to guide him to a quiet stop at the end of the driveway, went into the house through the kitchen. Light and television sound were apparent from the living room. He went the other way, down the hall toward his son's room. The door of the room was half open. He tiptoed in. The poodle jumped up in bed, recognized him, began wagging its tail.

"Tommy, are you asleep?"

"Yeah."

"It doesn't sound like you are."

"I ... I was. I'm kinda tired. I gotta game tomorrow."

"Sure, I know. It's late. I was at work."

"How come you always work late? Larry's father's home for dinner every night."

"Yeah, I know."

"We were talking about it. Most of my friends' fathers are home for dinner. I don't think I want to be in the advertising business if I have to work every night."

"Well, I guess what I do is different."

"How come?"

"Well, you've been to the office. You've seen all the ads we do, all the commercials."

"Yeah."

"Well, my job is to have the final say on all those ads before they go to our clients. I'm responsible."

"You mean you'd get fired if you didn't look at them?"

"Not really. Although, I guess if I didn't spend any time looking at the work, and the ads weren't any good, sooner or later I would be fired. But, it doesn't have anything to do with being fired."

"No?"

"No, it has to do with being responsible for something, trying to do the best you can. Understand?"

"I guess so."

O'Brien sat on the edge of the bed next to his son. He stroked the soft hair on the little poodle's neck. "It's like your Little League team. Mr. McGoldrick teaches each of you how to play better. That way the whole team improves. You can see that."

"Sure."

"Well, it's the same thing. If each ad gets a little bit better, the whole agency does, eventually."

"Yeah."

They sat in the darkness, silent. O'Brien sorted through his divorce explanation.

"Mom says you're going to lose the Global account. That's bad, isn't it?"

"I don't know where she got that idea. We've got some problems, but we're not going to lose the business." O'Brien held the boy's hand. "That's like baseball, too. When you pitch, you don't look at the batter and think, I wonder how far he's going to hit it. You think, what's the best way to get this guy out. Right?"

"Right."

"It's the same thing with Global. You have to believe you're going to win. If you don't, you lose."

He tucked him in, kissed him. "O.K., Tiger, get some sleep. I'll see you in the morning."

"Good night, Dad."

O'Brien went down the hallway a few steps to the guest bedroom where he would sleep. His last night in the house. He hadn't been able to explain to Tommy how he felt about the divorce, how he would try to be a good father, how he loved him more than anything else in his life, that he would do anything for the boy, but that he had a job, that life was more complicated than people realized, that you had to balance your priorities. He hadn't talked about any of it, although he'd planned it all out. He'd failed. The boy saw him as an absentee father, especially in comparison with his friends and their fathers. Helen, he was sure, didn't help much, and wouldn't help at all now. Based on her antagonism toward him and the fact that she'd hired a killer-diller lawyer there was every reason to believe she would make him look bad in front of his own son.

He'd had a whole game plan and none of it had come out. Tomorrow, he would be moving out, he wasn't sure yet to just where. He didn't know what he would be taking with him. He hadn't moved in twelve years. It was frightening, the thought of not having a home, not having a place to come home to after a long day at the office, after a business trip. Not being able to come home to his son and his dog. He was about to begin a life he'd only read about. He was the head creative person at the agency, in charge of the creation of innovative advertising, capable of anticipating the needs and desires of his fellow Americans. And here he was, confused about his own situation.

He'd made up his mind he'd wanted a divorce and now it was in the works. But, he hadn't understood all the implications, not just on the basics of where to live, but on his whole lifestyle, his relations with his neighbors, his community, his son. He'd told himself that his son was priority number one, but just now he'd not even broached the subject of what would be happening. Tomorrow, there was the Little League game. He made a vow he would talk to Tommy after the game, not bother him before. He would get up early and pack, try to do that without running into

Helen. He dreaded seeing her. He hadn't seen her since the fight the other night and he didn't relish another one. He wasn't very good at arguing and she was a champ. Besides, it didn't matter any more. What mattered was Tommy.

He wandered around the unfamiliar room, a stranger in his own house. He kicked at a loose pillow on the floor, missed and made contact with the edge of the bed. He sat down from the sharp pain in his ankle. It felt like it was beginning to swell. He thought of getting some ice for it, but didn't want to risk running into her. It hurt like hell to rub, but he did it anyway. His head ached, too. He sat back on the bed. He remembered a time when his parents had been away and he'd hurt his knee in a game, how much he'd missed them, how their being away and the pain made him cry. Was that how Tommy would feel when he left?

. . .

Harrison, New York

Murphy stood by the dresser, took the Colt 45 out of his briefcase, polished the handle with the end of his shirt. He slipped the cartridge out, double-checked to make sure there were no bullets.

"Every time I see you with one of those it makes me a wreck." She sat up in bed.

"It shouldn't, Maureen." Murphy walked across the bedroom. He reached up on top of the glass-paneled cabinet, found the key, opened the cabinet, carefully replaced the 45 next to the other pistols. "It should make you feel safe, knowing you're married to a crack army shooter."

"It's just that the boys are getting older and you know what can happen ... 'cause it does happen, all the time ... " She pointed at the TV.

"Those situations are about people who are sloppy. They own a gun, but they don't know how to take care of it, don't know how to keep it secure, don't even know how to shoot it." He examined himself in the mirror next to the gun case. His red hair stood out in stark contrast to his ashen pallor. He made a point to himself to get some sun if the weather was good over the weekend, or better yet, on his next trip to the island. It would be fun to take Regina to the beach ... to take her in the surf ...

In the mirror, Maureen was waving her arm to get his attention. "Why does someone your age have to play with guns? You'd think you'd outgrow them. He who lives by the sword ..."

"Some guys play golf, some tennis. Some guys collect coins. I like guns. And I like shooting them. It's my hobby. And, I'm damned good at it." He aimed a quick smile at her. He sat on the side of the bed, satisfied, slipped out of his Gucci's.

"Come to bed, you must be exhausted from all the travel and now this Global trouble." She reached for his hand.

He stood up. "I will ... in a minute. You know, you're right, I need to relax. I need to cool down from the pistol range. I think I'll watch a little TV downstairs, then I'll be up."

"You can watch here if you'd like."

"Thanks, but I just want to catch some of the Knicks. They're at home tonight."

She turned over in bed, got comfortable. "Now, there's a hobby, the Knicks... Basketball, period." She dismissed him with a half wave of her hand.

. . .

The fourth quarter was well underway. The Knicks were up by fourteen with six minutes to go. He had the Knicks by six. This should be easy.

A Miller Lite commercial appeared. He looked around the room, his favorite. If his father could see it. It had cost more for this room than any whole house his father had ever owned. Just the leather furniture.

He hit the mute button, returned the sound. The Timberwolves were on a run. Why did the Knicks always let the other team back into the game? What was this, democracy? Where were their killer instincts? "Come on, Oak," he said out loud. The Knick lead had dwindled to six, the same as the spread. Time out, Knicks.

His father, though poor most of his life, had been in many ways smarter than Malachy. Certainly, street smarter. Hanging around Ringling Brothers from an early age, moving all the time, fending for himself, had given him an advanced education in human behavior, at least at the lower levels.

"No," he yelled as Christian Laettner hit a three, reducing the lead to four with a minute to go. "Wake up, get with it!"

He couldn't sit. Three-thousand dollars about to be blown. "All right, Patrick," as the big center scored. The Knick lead was back to six. Milwaukee used their last time out. Most of the crowd was leaving the Garden, the game no longer in doubt.

Murphy paced back and forth. He could hardly breathe as Laettner tried another three from the corner. "Yes," he shouted as the ball bounced clear to mid-court, retrieved by Hubert Davis, who halfheartedly passed it ahead for a reverse lay up by a smiling Oakley at the buzzer.

"Yes, yes, yes!" A rush of exhilaration shot through his entire body. He pumped his right arm in the air, strode about the room, looked over at the large photograph of his father on the wall, pointed at it. "Yes!"

• • •

DAY 26

Bedminster, New Jersey

Saturday was not a day for baseball. But O'Brien knew, as he looked at the misting rain, that except for a deluge, they would get the game in. The schedule was short, over before the kids were let out of school for the summer. Games rained out were difficult to make up.

The temperature inside the house was chillier than outside based on his brief encounter with Helen when he was putting his things in the car. He had retreated to the guest bedroom and was planning on a quick escape to the Little League field as soon as he'd gathered the rest of his gear. Breakfast would be gotten on the way. Tommy would go to the game with some of his teammates.

He'd slept little. His ankle had throbbed. Looking back on the night, he was unable to distinguish the ugliness of his dream sequences from his wide awake thoughts, so dreary had they been. He could not remember being unhappier. His mind was unable to concentrate on any one subject for long. It boomeranged out of control from Global to divorce to Tommy and back again, the same black thoughts being played over and over.

The only pleasant ideas had occurred just before dawn and those had been about Sandy. Clay Walker was right about her. She was special, a pretty girl with a dramatic figure. If this was what the gym did for you, everyone should go.

Was Clay also right when he suggested that O'Brien had assigned this young woman to the Global shoot-out just so he could get closer to her? Clay saw everything in sexual terms. But, whatever his motivations were, he had to admit he was attracted to her, probably had always been attracted to her if he was completely honest with himself. Certainly, his musings that morning had been erotic. There was no denying that.

Although he and Helen hadn't gotten along, they had kept a modicum of a sex life. Helen had made sure of it. As with many segments of the marriage, she had been the aggressor when it came to sex. Looking back, it seemed until recently there'd been enough sex in the marriage. Enough to deter him from seeking anything outside. He wondered how some of his colleagues managed this sort of thing, assuming their bragging was based on some semblance of reality and not just a way to voice their masculinity to their buddies.

Clay was the exception, but there were others who carried on: had flings, affairs, even long term mistresses. O'Brien couldn't imagine where they found the time. In his case, not being home enough as it was, how could he have fooled around unless it was in the office, literally? His best friends kidded him about his hammock, begged him to tell stories. But, to him it was a place of escape and contemplation, somewhere to rest. How could people make love in a hammock anyway? He couldn't picture it.

His Catholic upbringing was a factor in all of this, too. When you are told over and over again that sex outside of marriage is forbidden, and that marriage is forever, it wasn't easy to forget.

Tommy poked his head into the room. "Dad, I'll see you at the game, my ride's here." He was gone as fast as he'd appeared.

"Great, Tommy, good luck, put it to those guys," O'Brien yelled after him. He grabbed his overnight bag and followed after his son.

. . .

O'Brien couldn't attend one of his son's games without being drawn back to when he was a Little Leaguer. He'd been good enough to make all-county in high school and then had played on the M.I.T. team. He would have liked to have coached Little League, but knew he wouldn't be able to deliver on the time commitment.

He waved across the field to another father, then stopped ... What was this? A familiar face was visible from the parking lot. A man headed his way.

"Father Joe, I can't believe it." It was his brother, a pastor of a church in Staten Island. It wasn't that far away, but his brother was busy too, so they communicated mostly by phone. That, plus the fact that Helen made his brother uncomfortable.

They embraced. "What brings you to New Jersey?"

"I talked to Tommy a couple of days ago. After all, he is my Godson. He told me he was pitching today. So, I decided to find out if he took after his father, or had real talent like his uncle.

Joe wasn't kidding about his pitching talent. He had his choice of scholarships, but chose the seminary instead. "Well, we'll see," said O'Brien. "Maybe he can pitch like you and hit like me."

"Let's check the old records. I'm willing to wager the second collection that I out hit you by a good twenty points." Father Joe waved at Tommy, who had taken the mound to face the first batter. "Give them the devil, Tommy."

"Fine language for a priest."

"There's nothing wrong with employing the forces of God in a good cause ... Give 'em the gas, Tommy."

O'Brien was figuring how to broach the other subject when his brother grabbed his arm. "Baseball's not the only thing Tommy and I talked about."

O'Brien darkened. He turned away from the action, measured his words.

"Look, I understand. Only too well. What do you think a parish priest deals with every day of his life?"

"I'm sure that's true ... You know, I had planned on calling you, but everything happened so fast. In fact, Tommy heard about it from Helen's mother before Helen or I could tell him."

"Everything's happening too fast these days and too young, too."

"I guess you see the world from its grittiest side."

"I do, but I see a lot of beauty and wonder, too. But, tell me what's happening with you. Is this for good? Can't you find a way to save the marriage? I can put you in touch with a counsellor, Dennis."

"It's too late for that. It's over. I moved out this morning, although I haven't figured out where I'm going to live. There are two lawyers hard at work, thanks to Helen and I."

"But, what about the boy?" He raised both his arms and yelled, "Way to go, Tommy." Tommy had struck out a big kid for the last out. The kid slammed down his bat and helmet just like the big leaguers he was mimicking.

"I'm torn up about him, can't sleep. He means so much to me, yet I'm doing the worst possible thing for him. Leaving. I've promised myself I'll make every effort to be with him, spend weekends on little trips, things like that."

"It's tough." He turned toward him. "You're a good man, Dennis, only a little too ambitious from my standpoint. I never could understand the fascination of Madison Avenue."

"You were lucky. I mean it, Joe. You got most of Mom's piety. I guess I got Dad's yearnings for power."

"It's not that simple and you know it. But, I can tell you from ample experience that Tommy needs a father at his age, someone to respect and someone to set limits. So, you'll have to figure a way to handle that. I know you will." He put his arm on his shoulder.

Tommy was back on the mound when the pager sounded.

"What's that?" said Father Joe.

"My pager, I'm sure it's nothing. I've got to call the office. We've got a crisis of sorts going on."

O'Brien walked to the car to use the phone. He recognized the pager number only too well. It was the agency chairman's assistant.

"Hi, Bea, it's Dennis. You called?"

"Hi, Dennis, yes, it's important. The chairman's called a meeting of department heads and others to discuss the implications of the Global problem. He wants to talk about some contingency plans. For example, he told me you should be developing a plan to cut a million dollars in salaries from the creative department." O'Brien gazed out at the field. Another batter, head down, returned to the dugout.

"Can you hear me, Dennis?"

"Did you say a million dollars?"

"Right. Anyway, he wants everyone to sit down and think this through while the news is fresh and there's still some time."

"Good, I'm in on Monday and will find the time to meet. Just let me know."

There was a stifled sound of amusement on the other end of the line followed by, "That's good Dennis, except the Chairman wants to meet today. Now, in fact. His schedule is wild next week. He's headed for the Far East tonight."

"Now? ... Gee, Bea, I'm at my son's Little League game."

"Is that what you want me to tell him? That Mr. O'Brien won't be coming, he's at a Little League game ... Look, Dennis, everyone I've talked to is being inconvenienced, it is Saturday after all. But, what can you do?"

O'Brien hesitated. He watched his son as he struck out another batter. "Bea, I'm about an hour's drive away, I guess, maybe less on a Saturday. I'm on my way."

He walked slowly back to where his brother stood. He loathed himself. He had just recommitted himself to his son and the next minute he was leaving. The worst was, there was no way to explain it. Either you understood the agency business or you didn't. Either you knew what an account like Global meant or you didn't. Either you understood his ambition to be president or you didn't. It couldn't be explained, not to his brother, certainly not to Tommy. He would have to find other ways to make it up to the boy.

"Joe, I've got to leave, a major problem at the office. My boss has called a meeting. Will you say goodbye to Tommy, tell him I'll call him later? I'll call you, too."

The priest studied him sympathetically, hugged him. "I will, Dennis, you take care. Be sure and call me later." He watched him go.

From the parking lot O'Brien thought he could see Tommy looking his way as he got into the car. He waved at him, but there was no response.

. . .

Luigi's Restaurant, Long Island, New York

Fran Irwin took a deep breath. "Smell the garlic. Dino, you don't know how good it smells in here."

"*Buono sera*, Mrs. Irwin, Mr. Irwin. It's good to see you. It's been a while since I see you. Come in, I've got a nice table for you in the back. Bruno will be your waiter." He led them through the crowded room to the rear of the restaurant. "Mrs. Irwin, where you been this time, the Caribbean, California? Sometime maybe you take me with you. Your husband no mind, eh?" He handed them menus.

"Sure, Dino, I'll call you, he won't mind." Fran gave her husband a light push, watched the owner return to the front of the restaurant.

"A Latin lover. He's probably not kidding. I wouldn't trust him."

"I love it when you get jealous."

"Well, I don't see enough of you. Dino's right, you do travel a lot."

"Larry, it goes with the job, you know that. You can't do sales promotion for an airline and not travel. We've been through that before."

"Tell me about what's going on, what's the latest with Baxter?"

"The latest is he's going full blast at what he does best, take advantage of his position. But, there's a new wrinkle."

"What's that?"

"The new president of Global, Bill Swenson. We had a meeting with him, the first one for me."

"What's he like?"

"He's tall, handsome, smart as hell, and on the case."

"How so?"

"He's only been directly in charge of advertising and sales promotion for a few days and he's already put Burns & Cody on notice."

"The advertising agency?"

"Right, and he said he wants to take a look at the companies that provide sales promotion."

"So, what's wrong with that?"

"Nothing at all, he's doing his job. In fact, it'll be interesting to see how much he gets into Maynard Baxter's bailiwick."

"How's Baxter reacting?"

"With his usual flip arrogance, the ugly little bastard."

"I'm sorry you have to work for him."

"Larry, no one would believe it, just let me tell you where he's been, or is going this year. The Super Bowl, Final Four, the

Masters, Indy, Wimbledon, the NBA finals, the Stanley Cup, wait, there's more ... "

He put his hand up. "Hey, I've heard all this."

"Can you imagine what it would cost for someone to maintain Baxter's life style? Every day, practically, somebody's entertaining him in some way. And the women!"

"Wait, here's Bruno. Bruno, it's good to see you."

"*Buono sera*, where you been so long?"

"Hey, Bruno, it's not me, she's the one who's away all the time. I could eat here every night."

"What you feel like, how 'bout some red wine? You like some Santa Margarita?"

"Great, and some appetizers." Fran smiled at Bruno.

"Fried zucchini for me, Bruno."

"*Due*, Bruno."

"*Due* zucchini coming up. I get your wine right away."

Larry tore the end off the hot loaf of bread Bruno had brought, passed the basket to Fran. "Now, are we going to have another Maynard Baxter tirade? It's not good for your digestion, Fran. The man's corrupt, what else can you say?"

"Evil is the only word to describe him. Talk about abusing your rank. And as I was saying, the women. Wherever we go these good looking bimbos emerge. The thought of going to bed with the little shit makes me ill."

"He's not Gregory Peck, but he's got something better. Power."

"He's got power all right, borrowed power, Global's budget of one-hundred-and-fifty million dollars for advertising and sales promotion. When you have that kind of dough everybody in the industry is after you to kiss your ass."

"Fran!"

"It's true. These customers want to take you to the best places. I know, I'm included a lot of the time."

"Isn't that part of the business? Haven't the media always entertained the clients?"

"Sure, and it's O.K. up to a point."

"What point?"

"The point you cross when you feel you owe them something back, when you forget it's not a social situation where maybe you do owe someone a dinner, that it's a business deal and the only reason they're taking you out is they want your business, your money. When you forget that, you start making decisions that are good for you, but not necessarily good for the airline."

"You've never done that."

"I don't know, I hope not. I try to make the best deals for the airline. But, a lot of people in the promotion business are my friends."

"People make friends in business all the time, what's wrong with that?"

"You know what I mean, Larry."

"All I know is you tell me Maynard Baxter takes advantage." The waiter brought the zucchini. Larry picked up a piece, blew on it to cool it. "Maybe this guy, Swenson, if he's so smart, will smell a rat."

"Don't you think I haven't thought of that? What happens if he does a complete investigation and finds out what's been going on? Suppose they incriminate me along with Baxter? I go on a lot of his junkets." She picked up a slice of bread, dipped it in the red wine. "And, there's worse stuff going on."

He put his knife down. "Worse. What's worse?"

"The airline's always selling vacation packages."

"Sure."

"More and more of those trips include condominiums rather than hotels as part of the deal. The condo owners compete like crazy to be part of Global's packages. It's the difference between a big season and a losing one for a lot of them."

"I can see that."

"Well, I think Baxter's been taking cash from some of them. I've never seen the money change hands, but I can see how decisions are being made and they're not always the best on the face of things."

"What kind of money are you talking about?"

"I don't know. Like I say, I've never seen any money on the table, but these deals are worth hundreds of thousands of dollars to the condo people, so they could afford some nice payoffs."

"And you're sure he's on the take?"

"Almost positive. Each trip things happen which make me suspicious. We just signed on with some apartments in Jamaica that weren't nearly as nice as some others on the island that would have cost the airline the same."

"This is heavy stuff."

"For sure, and I'm scared. If I blow the whistle they're likely to drag me into it. If I talk I'll be branded a corporate squealer, which would be the kiss of death to my career."

"So, maybe the smart thing is to keep doing the best job you can, keep your nose clean."

"I'm trying to do that, but it's not easy. I'm with Baxter a lot. I'm afraid I'll see something which I'll be forced to report. You know, in order to avoid being an accomplice."

He reached over and took her hand. "My God, Fran, I didn't know it was this bad, you must be going through hell. Maybe you should go to Swenson and tell him now, before he finds ... "

"But, Larry, I don't have any proof. So, Baxter's being entertained, that's just a question of degree. I can't say for sure he's being paid off. Do you think Swenson's going to be pleased to find out he has a scandal on his hands? The airline's got enough troubles as it is. I think I should do the best job I can and hope that Baxter makes a mistake, somehow hangs himself."

"You're probably right, but be careful. Promise me you'll tell me everything, even the things you don't think are important."

"I will, I need to tell somebody about it. Things are happening lightning fast. Which reminds me, one thing Baxter said to me does make sense."

"What's that?"

"He said if Swenson's going to fire the agency, a smart person would go along with him, because if he's going to become CEO of Global, which is what all the rumors say, he's going to remember who supported him."

"I have to agree. Hold it, here's Bruno. Let's not talk about Global anymore. It's time to enjoy the food. Bruno, how's the marinara supply? I'm starved."

• • •

DAY 24

Burns & Cody

Murphy rubbed his nose with the back of his hand, scanned Sparrow's office. Boring and safe, a perfect atmosphere for the agency's chief financial officer. You could feel secure that the agency's finances were in order. If people only knew. He looked up. Steve Sparrow joined Murphy in his office and shut the door.

"Hi, Steve, you look a little pale. What's up?"

"I just met with the chairman, Malachy. He's sending me as part of the first group to Outward Bound. I was never even in the Boy Scouts. Can you imagine?"

"A little fresh air will do you good."

"At this stage of my life I resent being sent to camp."

"If you save real hard you can retire early and no one will be able to tell you what to do."

Sparrow slumped into his chair. "Where's the money?"

Murphy opened his briefcase, took out several packets of bills, and placed them on Sparrow's desk. "I have some news. Part of our arrangement is changing."

"What's going on?"

"The Minister has raised the agency's billings to fifteen big ones. And his cut is going up proportionately. It's effective the first of the month."

"And our part goes up accordingly?"

"No." Murphy stood up, walked around the office. "Ours stays the same. He says we're getting plenty as it is. There's no need to change."

"I don't like the smell of it. Every other time this has happened, both shares have gone up with the billings."

"Which is what I said to him."

"And?"

"He said the agency was making a nice profit and we were getting a lot of money ourselves, so that's it."

"What do you mean 'we'? I thought ... "

"Don't get excited. He doesn't know about you, at least by name. He only knows there's somebody important involved from the financial side of the agency, that I couldn't get the checks to him on my own. He figured that out from the start. He's one smart cookie, and a tough one, too. Did I tell you he carries a gun around with him?"

"You did. I guess there's not much we can do."

"Do you know how often he reminds me there are plenty of agencies that would love to have his account? He's right, of course."

"Yeah."

"Another thing. I'm still laying off as many expenses as I can on the airline account, not much on tourism. It's important to make the San Sebastian profits look as good as possible, so no one gets suspicious."

"I wouldn't worry about that. I always point out to the executive committee at our profit updates that tourism is one of our more profitable accounts. It's a good thing you handle both clients. What's new on Global anyway?"

"We've only been on notice a week. On the other hand I haven't seen any new ideas. There are about three weeks left before our presentation. Meanwhile, we have to keep servicing the business as usual. There's a copy meeting over there tomorrow."

Sparrow placed the crisp packets in his attaché. "The money he gives us is always fresh." He held a packet up. "Even smells fresh."

"I thought of that. I don't trust him. Each month I take a few bills to the bank and have them checked out. They're good."

Sparrow shut his case. "I hope you are enjoying this. Don't bet it all on one game."

Murphy stiffened. "Don't talk like that. I enjoy a friendly wager from time to time. What's wrong with that? There are worse vices."

"From what I hear your bets are beyond the friendly kind. It's none of my business what you do with your share as long as you don't become too visible. People might wonder about somebody betting thousands on basketball games, might wonder where the money came from, a guy with a big mortgage and three kids."

"Where the hell are you getting all this? Sure I bet, but not that much and not that often. You're right, it's none of your business. I don't go around snooping into your personal life."

"It's hard to keep secrets around this agency. I only bring it up because if I know something, probably others do, too. Maybe you should be more circumspect. It's just good business."

Murphy reddened. He started to leave.

"Look, don't get your Irish up. Just be careful. This is a nice arrangement we have, the Minister's right about that. We don't want to spoil it."

"I won't. Remember you have the easy part of this deal, getting a check printed for the Minister once a month. I have the hard part, dealing with him on that island where he's practically king." He stood in the doorway, smiled. "Have a good time in the mountains if I don't see you before."

Once on the elevator Murphy felt better. Sparrow had gone along, hadn't suspected a thing. He pulled a sheet from his pocket, studied it. The Celtics, plus two at home against the Nets. That was the best bet, definitely.

. . .

Clay Walker ran down the hallway to the conference room. He slowed when he saw Sandy Stein inside standing by the big table in the center of the room.

"Hi." He peered around the room. "He's not here yet?"

"He's due any minute. You look a little harassed. Are you O.K.? What's that?" She walked around him to get a better look. "Did you hit your head on something?"

"Actually, something hit itself on me. I'll tell you about it after the meeting. I want to hear about the client before he gets here."

"I assume you've read all the background material."

"I have."

"Then you know the main problem is they're growing cranberries faster than America can eat them. We've worked with them over the years to create new ways to use them, like all the cranberry drinks, but there are still too many berries."

"But isn't most of the business cranberry sauce?"

"By far, but Thanksgiving and Christmas are only two days in the year. You can't invent new holidays. We had to find new eating occasions where somehow cranberry sauce would fit in. That's how we got the idea of a tie-in with chicken."

"Your idea?"

"It's kind of obvious. One night I was having dinner in this east side restaurant and the chicken I ordered came with cranberry sauce. A nice touch and it worked."

"The research says Americans eat fifty times more chicken than turkey."

"Right. When the client heard that, he got excited, as you will soon see. The idea we have today is all about chicken." She turned as a man entered the conference room. "Here's Barry now, right on cue. Barry, meet Clay Walker, your new head account man."

"Hi, Clay. Barry Noble. I read all about you in the letter your chairman sent us. Welcome to the business. It's a great time to come on, right Sandy? She must have told you about our chicken strategy. Do you realize if America served cranberry sauce with only ten percent of its chicken meals we'd double our business? Can you imagine?"

"We were just talking about it. That's why we ... "

"Wanted to tell you about a big idea we have." Sandy pulled out a chair for Noble. "We know you don't have much time, so sit over here, Barry, and let me get right into what we've come up with. We have a promotional idea that you're going to love. We've been looking for a big national promotion for late summer when cranberry sauce consumption is lowest and chicken is highest."

Noble nodded, took a pad and pencil from his briefcase, then looked up at Sandy.

"Listen to this. How would you like to have the biggest chicken of all time promote the idea of eating cranberry sauce with chicken? How would you like to see the most famous chicken ever, standing on a towering display of cranberry sauce in every supermarket in the country? How would you like to see a major cookbook featuring cranberry recipes endorsed by the country's cleverest chicken? How would you like to see every kid in America sending in cranberry sauce labels to get an inflatable doll of the most loved chicken in the United States?"

"I can't believe it, who is this chicken?"

"America's biggest, most famous, most loved chicken, Big Bird, from Sesame Street. We think it will be great for the kids. Lots of nutritional overtones. We haven't talked to them yet, but we think it's affordable, within your budget. It's all in this plan book. Now, Barry, wait till you see this."

"Hey Ben," Sandy called toward the rear door of the conference room. Moments later, a man entered the room with a four foot inflatable replica of Big Bird. He placed it on Barry Noble's lap, took out his card and handed it to him.

Noble read the card aloud.

Ben Barney
Balloons
BIG & small

"Ben's the world's biggest producer of balloons, Barry. By far. What do you think? Is this a big idea or what?"

Ben was on his knees looking up at Barry Noble, blowing additional air into a sagging Big Bird.

"This has to be the biggest promotional idea of all time. We're going to need a million of these."

"What?" Ben yelled. The huge chicken got away from him. The bird shot out of the conference room door like a balloon at a birthday party. There were screams from the corridor.

• • •

DAY 23

Burns & Cody

Sandy stood in the agency lobby waiting for them. Each time an elevator arrived she looked up. They were late. O'Brien had told her he wanted to introduce her to the people at Global now, rather than wait for the day of the final presentation. Today was just a routine day on the Global account, showing ideas to advertise a new route for the airline. O'Brien figured that by having Sandy in such meetings, the client would have time to get to know her, time to appreciate her potential value to them.

She took out her note again. She had written it to herself the evening before.

Be enthusiastic.
Be relaxed.
Be confident.
Be knowledgeable.

Below that were a half dozen points about the advertising she would be presenting.

Another elevator arrived. Still no O'Brien. Several of the people nodded to her as they passed. People she didn't know. Was it her imagination or were people all of a sudden greeting her? Were they aware of her new role? Did some of them understand that their jobs were in jeopardy at the end of the month unless the account was saved, unless this woman delivered? Perhaps that was too melodramatic. She put the note away.

Sandy looked down the lobby, studied the pattern in the stone flooring. Was O'Brien aware that this was the first time she'd been given a critical role on a big account? Had he reviewed her record? She seemed to be put on the smaller pieces of business, accounts where you couldn't do too much damage. Some of the small ones were fun, like the cranberry group. The client didn't overwhelm you with layers of people and processes. You could get a good idea through, like Big Bird. The idea might even be recognized around the agency. Mainly you weren't noticed on the small accounts unless something went wrong.

She had been fortunate. She had been cited for her work for a number of little clients and there had been no mistakes. But, great careers were launched or scuttled on the big accounts. That was where you made your mark if you wanted to make it to the very top. No one had gotten to the upper ranks of Burns & Cody without the visibility that went with succeeding on a big account.

Like Global, the biggest of the big.

Another elevator landed, empty. She looked at her watch, took out her crib sheet again. She still couldn't recite all the points without looking at the note. She might have to resort to leaving the note on the table during the presentation, although she knew it was more professional to have it committed to memory, to be able to naturally reel off the arguments like you had just thought of them. With conviction. She took out her pen and wrote,

Be convincing.

O'Brien, with Murphy behind, emerged from an opening elevator at a trot. She followed them onto Madison Avenue, where Murphy practically threw himself in front of a cab, screeching it to a halt.

"Everybody squeeze in the back so we can look at the advertising," said O'Brien. He held the door for Sandy.

"How come I never get to see the work before we present it to the client?" asked Murphy.

"Because it's 1995 and it's the agency business and we have an unstable client, and when I tried to get hold of you, you were in San Sebastian again. By the way, Malachy, Sandy is going to present the advertising today."

As the cab took the short ride to Rockefeller Center and the Global building, Sandy leaned over and held up a layout. "Malachy, the first approach is straight forward airline advertising. It tells the story fast with no embellishments. The headline, 'Now, Two Non-stops to Roanoke' works well with the illustration of the two Global jets with their departure times underneath them.

"Now, here's an alternative. The headline, '76 Reasons to Go to Roanoke and the 2 Fastest Ways to Get There' plays off the 76 pictures of different people and places in Roanoke. We put the detailed information about he Global flights in this mortise in the corner of the ad. What do you think?"

"I like the first one. It tells the flyer what he needs to know. It's got big Global identification, which the sales people will like, and it won't cost much to produce, which the one with all the pictures will."

O'Brien reached over and took the second layout from Sandy. "We think this could be a prototype for a broader campaign, showing local people and places around the Global system. There could be an ad for every key city. It has a lot of local interest, and it's filled with civic pride possibilities. And it will stand out from the other airline advertising, which is pretty bland and boring. Like the version you like, Malachy."

"I still like the first one better, we should recommend it."

"Look, Malachy, I don't want to pull rank on you," said Sandy, "but the chairman is getting stats of everything we do on

Global these days and he called me out of the blue to say how fresh he thought the second approach was."

"That settles that," said O'Brien. "Now, tell us, Malachy, who's going to be there today from their side?"

Murphy grimaced, stared out the window.

O'Brien reached for his arm. "Look, Malachy, don't get so touchy all of a sudden. What's new about arguing over an ad? It happens all the time ... Now, tell us who's going to be there."

Murphy turned toward them. "Jack Kreeger, maybe Ted Crowther. Crowther's the airline's marketing director, Sandy. A good guy, smart, and a friend of the agency. Most likely, just the two of them."

"Here we are," said O'Brien. He let Murphy out, then helped Sandy from the car. As she slid across the seat, her legs drew attention despite her efforts to cover them. She pulled on her skirt. O'Brien stood there, transfixed. He looked up at her, embarrassed that she had seen him staring. He moved to close the door.

Sandy studied his face. He had actually become red for a split second. Was it her imagination or had he looked at her that same way the day she had been given the assignment to head up the Global effort? She liked the idea that he might be interested. And that he was shy about it like a little boy.

. . .

Global Airlines Building, Rockefeller Center

"This building," said Murphy, "has more security than the Pentagon."

"True," said O'Brien, happy for the distraction. "Sandy, it's something you will have to get used to. They treat the building as though it's a large airliner and every visitor's a potential high-jacker. You can't get in without a Global employee meeting you, and it's even harder to get out."

They went through security with the help of Kreeger's secretary. The Global building, its offices, and especially its main conference room struck Sandy as lavish in light of the company's economic problems. Obviously, this had been done during brighter times.

The clients were already in the room when they arrived so O'Brien took no time in introducing her and starting the meeting. Sandy took one last glance at her note. She went through the two versions of advertising, pointed out the arguments for the recommended one. Finished, she turned to Jack Kreeger for a response.

Kreeger remained silent, unable to think of anything to say about the work. He stared at the top of the table, toyed with his pencil. He looked up at them, started to speak, hesitated ...

The group was getting impatient with Kreeger's slow response. He looked back into his lap. His hands were firmly wrapped around his ears as he concentrated.

Finally, Ted Crowther saved him. "I like the second version. It's innovative. We'll review it with sales and get back to you as soon as possible. I think the agency did an excellent job. Thanks for coming over." He stood, smiled, left the room. Kreeger followed him.

O'Brien turned to Sandy. "Nice going. One copy meeting, one sale."

"I can't believe the ignorance of Kreeger. How could they make him advertising director?" said Murphy as he helped O'Brien gather up the layouts, placed them back in the carrying case.

"Malachy, I want you to try and find out something," said O'Brien. "How did Kreeger get his position? Was he brought in by Swenson, for example. He may be stupid, but he's got a vote. Let me know what you find out, will you?"

He noticed the dour looks on his two cohorts. "I'm not worried, it's just prudent to keep track." He wished he completely believed what he had just said.

. . .

Fran Irwin didn't know what to expect from her meeting with Swenson. In her fifteen years at Global, her whole career, she had rarely been in the same room with the president of the airline. Now, in less than a week she was having her second meeting with one. Only in this case it would be just the president and her. The phone call from Swenson's secretary told Fran little about the nature of the meeting. Fran had responded to Swenson's request for a report on Global's sales promotion suppliers by staying up half the night to compile as quick and as comprehensive a dossier as she could. She assumed this is why she had been called. Yet a meeting like this brought to the surface the constant fear of exposure that lurked underneath all of her activities with Baxter.

The problem with Baxter had been evident since she first went to work for him directly five years before. His constant gallivanting and socializing with the media were obvious. Yet, to Fran his activities had worsened over time. Lately, Baxter didn't seem to show any discretion whatsoever, particularly when it came to women. And, then there were the kickbacks. A man like Swenson wouldn't take kindly to Baxter's behavior if he knew about it.

But, the chances of his becoming aware were slim. Only if someone were to blow the whistle. Fran had decided she would not be that person. There was too much to lose from such action and little to gain. Even if her accusations were proven accurate and Baxter was fired as a result, Fran's reputation would be damaged permanently. And people would point out that she, too, was guilty of being over-entertained. After all, she was with Baxter on almost all of his trips.

Fran didn't, on principle, believe in ratting on people. Whenever there was a cheating scandal at one of the military academies she had trouble understanding why students were discharged because they failed to report their fellow students for cheating. She didn't think cheating should be allowed, but she felt it wasn't right to blame bystanders simply because they had remained silent. At any rate, this wasn't West Point, although Swenson seemed to treat Global like it was.

What made the Baxter situation untenable was the likelihood that he had escalated his bad deeds to a much higher level. Fran was convinced he was receiving kickbacks from island condo owners. Importantly, she had not witnessed such behavior. If she had, her theories on ratting would be tested. It was one thing to live the good life thanks to the airline's media suppliers. But, taking payments from airline condo owners was in an entirely bigger league. That was Federal offense material, she was sure.

Could Swenson be on to this? Was that the purpose of the meeting? When she had told Baxter she was meeting with the president one-on-one, he had gone pale. All the bravado disappeared. Normally, he made light of everything, but underneath he must be worried about Swenson, too. He had ordered her to call him immediately after the meeting, told her to take comprehensive notes of everything Swenson said.

She wished the man would hurry. She had thought about nothing else but the meeting from the moment his secretary had called. The last thing she needed was a postponement. She got up, walked to the secretary's alcove just as he arrived.

"Sorry, Fran, bankers. You have no idea how much time I spend with bankers. I thought I had left the banking industry, gone into a broader management position. But, instead of dealing with the operation of the airline, I seem to spend my time reassuring the bankers that their loans are good."

"Are they?" She surprised herself at the boldness of her inquiry.

"I tell them not to worry, so they better be." He reached into a drawer, took out her report. "I was very impressed by this. So fast and so complete. For someone who knew nothing about sales promotion I now feel comfortable about what we are doing. I wanted to ask you a couple of questions, though."

"Sure." She got out her pen and note pad.

"First, it would appear that you always get three competitive bids, no matter what the assignment. Is that true?"

"Absolutely. Once in a while when the job is so specialized and there's only one or two suppliers available we don't, but that's a rare occurrence."

"Good. Also, I want to be assured that we are not becoming too dependent on any one or two suppliers. Familiarity breeds contempt in my book."

"Well, we've had some long-time relationships, say with the printer of our airline schedules, but we still get three bids every year. And, if we have a big contract, say for our winter travel agent promotions, I try to break the job into smaller pieces."

"I like what you're saying. That is, I believe you have the right attitude. Now, tell me about these condo promotions with the islands."

She wondered if he had noticed how her arm trembled. She quickly folded her hands together, put them in her lap. Was this what he was driving at the whole time? Reassuring her to set her up for the kill? "What is it you'd like to know, sir?"

"The same kind of thing. Do we get three bids? Do we over rely on any suppliers? Do we have long term relationships?"

"Our arrangements with the condo owners are made by Maynard Baxter. I help in the pre-screening. On some islands there may be as many as ten possible suppliers and as many as three that we actually sign on. That would be true with the big destinations like Bermuda and Jamaica. With the smaller islands there may not be much choice. It varies."

"I see, I'll make a note to ask Mr. Baxter about it when I see him. This is big business for us, these vacation packages. I want to be confident we're doing it as efficiently as possible. Just like with everything else." He stood up, put out his hand.

His grip was firm, reassuring. Fran wondered what his wife was like. "Thanks, Mr. Swenson. Is there anything further you'd like me to do?"

"Not that I can think of. Of course, we'll continue to have our regular meetings: you, Mr. Baxter and Jack Kreeger. One-hundred-and-fifty million dollars is one hell of a lot of money to spend on advertising and sales promotion. We damned well better be doing it right."

• • •

DAY 22

P.J.'s

O'Brien slid into the booth across from his friend. "How's it going?"

"Great. How's the agency's favorite account?"

"I put on a good face, but the truth is, we have twenty-two days to go and we don't even have a theme line. How can you have a complete advertising campaign in twenty-two days when you don't have a theme line? It's terrifying."

"That's not good." Clay looked over at Yogi Berra, whose back was turned.

"Plus, when this thing started, we had thirty days and everyone said, 'Gee, thirty days, that's only 4 weeks and a few days.' Well, that's not true."

"It's not?" He still couldn't make eye contact with the bartender.

"No, people forget that Saturdays and Sundays count and so does the Monday of Memorial Day Weekend, so when you add it all up it's more like twenty working days. Some people are going to have to come in on weekends pretty soon."

Clay finally got Yogi's attention, ordered a single Cutty. "Really? Well, I can tell you some of the people are already working weekends. The joke going around is, 'If you don't come in on Saturday don't bother coming in on Sunday.'"

"It's a tough time for the agency, but if we don't keep the account lots of people won't have to worry about coming in, period."

"Pretty grim."

"Let's not talk about what could happen. Let's talk about something else."

"There is one thing I wanted to ask you about, how's the divorce situation?"

O'Brien leaned forward, both elbows on the table, his chin in his hands. "It's a nightmare."

"Tommy?"

"That's part of it, but I meant the lawyers."

"I hate lawyers."

"Well, in this case, Helen has adopted a scorched earth policy. But, it seems to me that my lawyer, while he complains about the tactics of Helen's lawyer, is secretly enjoying what's happening."

"How so?"

"Well, I get the impression he likes the way it looks, like a long, slow fight to the death. They get paid by the hour, you know."

"No, shit!" Clay raised his voice in mock surprise.

"It could be expensive."

"Are you crazy, these guys will take you to the cleaners. They probably call each other up at the end of the day and laugh their little evil hearts out."

"Wouldn't that be collusion, or something?"

"Boy, are you naive. You better pay attention or you won't have anything left when they're through with you."

"Like I've got time for this right now."

"You look frazzled, I think you need a date with a sweet young thing. What about Sandy, did you do what I said?"

"The timing is not right, but ... "

"But, what?"

"Nothing."

"What do you mean nothing? What were you going to say?"

"I do like her, I will ask her out, but not till the Global problem's been resolved."

"But, you were going to say something else a minute ago."

"Well, I was, something personal ... I was going to ask you for some advice."

"Sure, what is it?"

"I assume we always talk in confidence."

"You bet, what is it?" Clay squinted at O'Brien.

"This is ridiculous ... It's a long time ... you know, since I dated anyone, but since this divorce got started my attitude toward women has changed."

Clay moved forward in his seat, smiled. "Yes?"

"Well, maybe it's not my attitude. I'm not sure what it is, except I'm more aware of them."

Clay threw his hands in the air. "Good God, there's hope for civilization."

"You don't understand, as a married man I didn't look at women as potential mates. I was married. Anyway, I'm particularly aware of Sandy, drawn toward her. Like the song says, 'she's always on my mind.' I've liked her as a person all along and she's very attractive, but because of Global we're spending a lot of time together and I find my mind wandering, having fantasies about her."

Clay looked off into space. "This is good. The man's in lust."

"Maybe. Maybe, it's something else."

"You don't lust?"

"Sure."

"Look, do you want to jump on her bones or don't you?"

O'Brien shook his head. "You're such a romantic. The answer is, I'm very attracted to her. But, I think about her in other ways than sex. I enjoy being with her."

"Well, you could be falling in love, something I'm not into. I focus on lust. I found love calamitous."

"I'm sorry to hear that. What happened?"

"It led to marriage."

"I'm serious here. What's the way to tell the difference, lust versus love?"

Clay was silent. He toyed with his glass. "But love is blind, and lovers can not see the pretty follies that themselves commit."

"Robert Burns?"

"Shakespeare, The Merchant of Venice."

O'Brien grimaced. "But, love versus lust?"

"O.K., first thing is, you can't love a woman as far as I'm concerned unless you lust for her. But, you can certainly lust for a woman without loving her. That's my area of concentration. If I were you I'd stay in the lust area for a while, until you get used to being single. My God, you could go from marriage to marriage and skip the fun altogether. That would be tragic."

"Sometimes I can't tell how much you're kidding."

"I'm not kidding. When it comes to women and me, lust is fine. And I don't kid around with women about it either. I'm not one of these guys who goes around with flowers, promising to leave my wife because I'm so in love. That's dangerous business, no matter what your motives are."

"It seems like a game to you."

"You got it. It beats any other game you can name."

"The point is, I'm realizing more and more that I care about Sandy. When we're together I'm happy, and when we're not together, I'm thinking about when I'm going to see her again." He stared past Clay toward the bar.

Clay leaned back, folded his arms across his chest. "Well, here's my advice. First, to ask her out; second, to get some fine wine; third, to tell her how you feel about her; and after that even you should have no trouble."

"You think?"

Clay leaned back. "I can't believe it. You are the smartest, most creative person I know, but sometimes I ... "

"Let's just say I'm out of practice." O'Brien checked his watch, jumped up from the booth. "I'll see you, I've got to go back to the agency. We've got two groups presenting Global ideas." He dropped a ten dollar bill on the table, headed toward the door.

Clay watched him go, then yelled, "Do it!"

• • •

DAY 21

Fifth Avenue

As the limo headed south, Swenson watched Kreeger out of the corner of his eye, kept the *Wall Street Journal* in front of him. Kreeger reminded Swenson of the character, Lenny, in the movie *Of Mice and Men.* Dumb, but well meaning, sort of lovable. Most of all, for Swenson's immediate purposes, malleable.

"Look, Jack, when we get to Burns & Cody I'd like you to listen. Try not to talk except if you'd like to support me. The airline should speak with one voice. This is an important meeting, my first at the agency. I want to hear what they have to say. The board wants us to have the best agency available. They believe advertising is critical to the success of the airline. We spend a bundle on it, so it better work. But, my entire background is finance. I need to learn about advertising."

"I heard you were the youngest executive vice president ever at Citibank."

"That's true, Jack, I was 35. Hard for me to believe that was only two years ago." He took a comb from his back pocket and ran it through his hair. He handed the paper to Kreeger. "Have you seen this?" He stretched back in the seat, his head against the head rest, his eyes closed. "I've got some thinking to do."

Swenson ran through the issues facing the airline. Most related to money, keeping the system afloat until business improved. If Global could be one of the survivors in a better economy they could coin money.

He opened his left eye enough to look at Kreeger. Kreeger had adopted an identical position to his, head back, eyes closed. Swenson smiled. Whatever happened with the agency situation he would find a spot for Kreeger. Something he could handle, perhaps another sales job. Meanwhile, he had someone he could control, a vote in his pocket. He felt he had the support of Maynard Baxter as well. And it seemed to him that Fran Irwin would do whatever Baxter asked. With his own vote, that added to four, a clear majority.

Burns & Cody meant nothing to him personally. But, they were a factor in the battle for control of the airline. To the extent that the agency was tied to Global's chairman, Haps Corwin, they were a vestige of the old order, the order that had nearly bankrupted the airline. He was the new order. The enlightened members of the board could see that. If he was going to oust Corwin and become chairman he would have to exert control. The agency could be an example of that.

Today, Swenson decided to enjoy himself. It was rare that he found himself in a business meeting where numbers were not the critical issue.

The limousine pulled up in front of Burns & Cody. "Here we are, Jack."

Kreeger, who had his hands over his ears, pressed against his head, could not hear Swenson.

"We're here, Jack!"

Kreeger dropped his hands, looked out the window. "This is it, Mr. Swenson."

They walked the short distance to the agency entrance. "Jack, I sent you a reminder letter about the second agency. Did you get it?"

"Yes, sir, I am working on a recommendation."

"Good. Also, you should be aware that from time to time we may run ads that have to do with financial matters: takeovers, mergers, LBO situations, that kind of thing. I want you to schedule a meeting with my secretary to talk about these. This is a very timely and extremely secret subject."

"Yes, sir, here's our floor."

Swenson followed Kreeger down the hall into the conference room. He was surprised to find just three people from the agency. He looked around expectantly. A medium sized, athletically built man stepped forward, introduced himself.

"I'm Dennis O'Brien. I wanted us to have a small, informal meeting, Bill, a chance to discuss where we've been. Malachy Murphy, here, has run the Global account for five years. He's the most knowledgeable person about everything the agency's done. Over here, Sandy Stein is the new day-to-day creative director on your business. I wanted you to meet her. She'll be part of the comprehensive presentation we'll be making in a couple of weeks. As for myself, I'm the creative director of the agency. I've always been active on the Global account. Brad Burns, our chairman asked me to apologize for his not being here. He's in China, as I believe he told you."

O'Brien led Swenson to a seat as Murphy got up and walked to the other side of the big round table, the centerpiece of the room.

"Let me start with a brief background of our relationship with Global," said Murphy. "And relationship is the key word, because Burns & Cody and Global have been true business partners."

"That's a cardinal business principal," said Swenson.

"Cardinal," said Kreeger, nodding his head.

O'Brien and Sandy presented representative advertising from previous Global campaigns. Murphy provided intermittent business perspective.

"I didn't realize most of what you do has a sound strategy behind it," said Swenson. "That makes sense."

"It does," said Kreeger.

"That last TV commercial reminded me of my small hometown in Texas," said Swenson. "You've captured the emotions perfectly."

"Emotional," said Kreeger.

Everyone looked at Kreeger. Swenson regretted his earlier instructions. He decided to confine himself to questions for the rest of the meeting.

An hour later, back in the car, Swenson mused about the presentation. "I was impressed by that group, very professional. With it. It would be too bad to fire them, but I guess that happens all the time on Madison Avenue. Agencies fired for reasons having nothing to do with advertising." He looked over at Kreeger, expecting his agreement, but Kreeger had his hands over his ears again, oblivious to Swenson's words. Swenson shook his head, leaned back, smiled.

• • •

DAY 20

Burns & Cody

Murphy shut the door to his office, sat down at his desk, took out a writing pad. He wrote "Assets" at the top, penciled in the numbers underneath from memory. He held the pad up, double-checked the amounts.

ASSETS $(000)	
House	800
Stocks & Bonds	400
Burns & Cody stock	525
Cash	75
Life Insurance	500
Total	2300

Next, he wrote "Liabilities," and proceeded to list them.

LIABILITIES	
Mortgage	400
Burns & Cody loan	175
Auto loans	25
Total	600

This exercise was reassuring. To see he was, in fact, a millionaire, even without the company life insurance policy. If only his father were alive. He would be astounded by Murphy's success, something his father had not come close to.

He tore the sheet off, turned it over and wrote "Income" at the top, made a list.

INCOME	
Salary	180
Bonus	50
Interest/dividends	30
San Sebastian	125
Total	385

Underneath, he listed his expenses.

EXPENSES	
Mortgage payments	37
Real estate taxes	15
Household	75
Income taxes	105
Burns & Cody loan	15
Total	247

He studied the numbers. The importance of his deal with the Minister was apparent. Without that income, his expenses would be about the same as his income.

He crumpled the sheet and threw it away, tore off a clean sheet and wrote "Wins & Losses, May." From his desk drawer he took a clipped file of penciled notes. He transferred the data to the sheet of paper.

WINS & LOSSES, MAY

WINS	
5/3 Lakers	1000
5/6 Bullets	2500
5/11 Nuggets	750
5/27 Knicks	3000
Total	7250
LOSSES	
5/1 Knicks	500
5/8 Bulls	1000
5/14 Celtics	2500
5/19 Suns	5000
5/23 Bulls	7500
5/24 Knicks	5000
Total	21500

He subtracted the difference. He'd lost $14,250 in less than a month. By far, his worst month ever. April had been a losing month, too. He was due for a turn around.

He picked up the phone, pushed the intercom. "Hold all calls, please."

He went over to the couch that ran along the wall by the windows in his office, and stretched out. The Global situation worried him. While he still headed the account, he was not as involved in the agency's efforts to save the business as he felt he should be. His worst fear was that they were thinking of replacing him on the account. That would be devastating. It would leave him with just the San Sebastian account to run, not enough to justify his financial package.

At fifty, he was vulnerable. At that age, anyone in the business was vulnerable unless they were at the very top echelons of the agency. He had seen the pattern over the years. You work hard for twenty-five years, get to run some big accounts, finally get the big salary and bonus and some company stock. Then the agency, any agency, finds someone younger with half the salary to take your place. What they might lack in experience they compensate for with enthusiasm and energy. When they replace you, the client might complain, but a few weeks later you're forgotten.

In the Global situation it wouldn't be crazy for the agency to think of putting a fresh face on the business. They'd already introduced Sandy Stein as the new creative head of the account for that very reason. New, young blood.

If it came to that and he was reduced to running one account, someone would soon figure out he was unaffordable, that it would be better to give him a reasonable kiss off, a year's salary maybe. That would be the end of his payoff from the Minister.

The Minister, the prick, would laugh at that. Until he realized it might not be so easy to find another Murphy for his scam. Not many agency executives would be bold enough to go along with the Minister. Some would blow the whistle at even a hint of corruption.

The Minister didn't know the name of the financial partner Murphy was working with. Steve Sparrow thought that Murphy had held his name back to protect Sparrow, but to Murphy it was a small piece of insurance against the Minister, his not knowing the other Burns & Cody man in on the deal, the man who actually got the checks printed and sent to the island. That was a plus for Murphy.

If he was in jeopardy at the agency it might be a good time to have a conversation with the Minister, talk about moving the account, lock, stock and barrel to a brand new agency. He would wait for an opportune time to present the idea to Ramon, it wasn't necessary yet. It could be that he was imagining too much, that he was secure at Burns & Cody no matter what happened with Global or if they ...

His buzzer interrupted. "I thought I asked that all calls be ..."

"I know, Mr. Murphy, but there's a man named Yogi on the line. He won't tell me why he wants to talk to you, but he says it's urgent, he wouldn't give up."

"It's O.K., Helen, put him through."

"Christ, Yogi, what's going on? I told you not to call me at the office." Murphy could hear the clatter of P.J.'s in the background.

"Look, Murph, the boys are getting itchy. You're down twenty-five large. That's the most you've ever owed. They're not Chase Manhattan, you know. And you're not the fucking government of Brazil."

"I was planning on coming by on my way to the train. Tonight. In fact, within the hour. I'll be there." Murphy heard a grunt from Yogi before the line went dead. He changed lines, got a dial tone, pushed the first memory button.

"Hi, Maureen. It looks like I'll be able to make the 7:10. Maybe we could go out for a bite, get a sitter for the kids or something."

"That would be great, Malachy. I've been locked up with them forever."

"Good. The other thing is I've been thinking and I don't see why we can't send the kids to camp this summer. It would be good for them to get away, see a little of the world, and it would be good for you."

"Why, Malachy, that's a wonderful idea. A couple of the girls today were saying how they weren't looking forward to the kids getting out of school, having them under their feet all summer. Do you think they are old enough to handle it?"

"No problem. I remember going to a Boy Scout camp where they had five-year-olds. It'll teach them some independence. We'll talk about it when you meet the train. I'll see you then. I've got one more meeting."

Murphy crossed the room, bolted the door. He closed the blinds on his windows, unlocked his closet, removed the briefcase. He punched in his security code, opened the case. He counted out twenty-five thousand and placed it in an envelope, sealing it. He put the envelope in his everyday attaché case, decided to go straight to P.J.'s.

He headed down the hallway, ran the last few steps to catch an elevator.

"Hey, Red, what's the matter? You don't say hello to your friends?"

Murphy looked up. "Sorry, Harry, I guess I was thinking about something."

"Probably the airline, huh? How's it going on that anyway?"

"No problem. Just a little review. The new president's checking out all of their suppliers."

The elevator opened into the lobby. The friend left, reassured. Murphy shook his head. The whole agency was uptight. He smiled at a couple of art directors that he knew, went out into the street. He was glad he had come up with the camp idea. Maureen deserved it, she was a good wife. It wasn't her fault that she didn't turn him on like the old days. Turn him on like Regina did. No one had ever excited him as much as Regina. He had worked hard all his life. He deserved some fun. No one would ever know, so what was the problem. His wife was happy, the kids were happy.

. . .

P.J.'s

He edged his way up to the busy bar, looked for Yogi, spotted him at the end. Yogi was waving at Clay Walker at a booth back in the corner of the room. He could make out O'Brien in the booth with Walker. Yogi turned back, responding to an order at the bar. Finally, the bartender saw him and came over. He shook his hand and took the envelope in one swift motion, placed it under the bar. He whispered, "Is that the whole twenty-five?"

"That gets me even. Now it's my time to score. Give me five on the Bulls. It's plus five in the paper."

"It just went to four-and-a-half. You could use the half point the way you've been rolling. You sure you want five? That's heavy duty for you."

"I'm due, I can feel it. Yogi. I'm about to launch a winning streak, you watch."

"I'll be watching. And so will they. They don't like folks that get behind."

"I'm going to build up a fat credit balance here so that they won't have to worry." He turned to leave.

"Good luck," called Yogi Berra. "I think you're going to need it."

• • •

DAY 16

Burns & Cody

O'Brien walked to the window, parted the blinds. It was just beginning to become light. To most, it was a new day, to him it meant one less day. He crossed his office to the opposite wall, where a display had been hung. Sandy had given it to him, one of those butcher shop numbering systems. You take a number and wait your turn, except in this case, instead of the numbers going up, they went down. He removed several sheets, revealing the number 16.

The past weekend had been the bleakest period in his life. Ten days ago he had moved into the Doral Hotel, on Park Avenue, not far from the agency. His original plan had been to find an apartment, but he'd been shocked at the cost of the only decent places available in the neighborhood of the agency. And he was unprepared for the long term commitment he would have to make to obtain a desirable space. After a few days of investigation he'd decided to arrange to stay at the Doral, at least until the presentation was over.

His absorption in agency activities during his first week in the city overshadowed his new lifestyle. But, the long Memorial Day weekend just past caught him off guard. It seemed that he was the only one in New York without a plan. Off and on, bored and by himself, he'd gone over to the agency in the hope of accomplishing something on Global, but had found few people working. On Memorial Day the office had been empty.

The silence of the normally buzzing agency had made him yearn for people contact, something to do. Back in the street, his loneliness was exacerbated by the bustle and pace of the city. Everyone seemed to be part of a group, and a festive group at that. He'd found it ironic that he could be lonesome in the midst of many. He'd missed Tommy more than ever, wondered what he was up to. No doubt he and Helen had gone to the neighborhood cookout, a Memorial Day ritual. Would Tommy be the only boy there without a father?

Leaving the baseball game in the middle of it the week before had unnerved him. He had reached his son by phone that Saturday night, learned that he had pitched a shutout, but the conversation had been brief and unfulfilling. After all, O'Brien hadn't been there to the end. Now, not being around on a holiday elevated his guilt.

On one level he loathed himself for his self pity. Yet, he felt that he was being victimized by his own success. What was wrong with trying to succeed? He'd worked hard and now he was at a point where he could attain the summit, if only a few things went his way. Being president of the agency was crucial to him. After that, he would have greater control over his life. After that, he would be able to make it up to Tommy.

That's assuming they kept the Global business. If they didn't, he would have to fire a fourth of the creative department. The Burns & Cody reputation would be marred, diminishing the chances of winning new accounts. The agency's finances would be in disarray. A healthy, prosperous concern would become unprofitable. Those who managed to keep their jobs could forget about raises, forget about bonuses. His own name would lose its aura. He would not be made president. He couldn't imagine all of this happening on top of his personal dilemma.

He forced his attention to the papers on his desk. As was his habit first thing each morning, he compiled a list of the agency's creative priorities. He didn't need to write down the name of the airline. Instead, he wrote down the names of a dozen other clients along with their needs. The problems encompassed the spectrum of components that comprised an advertising campaign. Here, the need to develop a radio version of an established campaign. Here, the need to make contemporary the music of an old campaign. Here, the need to keep the main elements of a campaign, but to change the theme line because a competitor had pointed out to the FTC the possible illegality of the client's claim. Here, the need to develop an entire back-up campaign because the client felt his advertising was worn out. Clients got sick of their advertising long before consumers did.

He wondered why the untidiness of it all didn't unravel him. You could satisfy one client one day, but the list never shrank. The same client, or another one, had a new idea on how to improve his advertising. Just when you thought the list of demands was going to break the back of the agency, something would be added.

A month before, he and the chairman had spent a day at Heritage Village, north of the city, sorting out the needs of all the clients, evaluating the forces the agency had to bring to bear against them, discussing how to strengthen their resources to increase the quality of the writers and art directors, but within tight cost restrictions. It seemed a tough, but manageable job. Then, Global had struck.

Everything in his pre-advertising life had been orderly. The whole Roman Catholic dogma, being an altar boy within a liturgy that never changed. Four years at M.I.T. seeking solutions to the third decimal point, Q.E.D. Except for Viet Nam, the Marine

Corps had been a bastion of precision and neatness. Even amid the craziness of war there was a residual semblance of Corps order that underlined events.

Looking back, the entirety of his past belied the possibility that he could be happy in a business that produced a product that was incapable of measurement, one that no one ever knew the true value of, a product whose creation relied on the collaboration of a collection of talented, unpredictable, and often neurotic individuals.

Over the weekend he had been on the verge of calling Sandy at home. He was surprised how much he missed her, how much he yearned for her company, her energy. She had stayed calm and upbeat even though time was running out. Her confidence helped his.

On both Sunday and Monday he'd wandered by her office several times looking for her. If she'd been present, there was the possibility that he could have extended their talk about Global into going somewhere afterwards, perhaps to dinner.

The more unavailable she was, the more he'd convinced himself he had to be with her. And when she hadn't shown up either day, (he was sure of this because he'd checked the agency's sign-in sheets with the security people), he began to wonder if Clay was wrong, that in fact she had a boyfriend and had gone away with him for the long weekend.

He was sure she would be in the office today. He checked his watch to see if it was too early to call. It was 8:00 a.m. exactly. He needed to see where they stood on Global. So far, in two weeks, no advertising ideas had surfaced as worthy of pursuit. Perhaps a few fragments here and there, but nothing big. No one had suggested a campaign theme of any substance. He would have to turn the screw another notch.

He put the list of projects on the table next to the hammock, reached for the phone just as the intercom sounded.

"Charlie Shapiro's on line two, he's found Clay Walker. And, I need money for stamps. Oh, there was a call from your lawyer, Tony Wainwright. Said it was urgent."

O'Brien sat up, pushed the two button. "Charlie, what's the story?"

"I found him," said Shapiro. "He's in Boston."

"What's he doing in Boston?"

"They had a cranberry meeting down on the Cape on Friday. When they got back to Boston, Clay had a few drinks and decided to look up an old girlfriend. I guess he got a six-pack and a taxi and eventually got to this lady's house in Chestnut Hill, which was too bad."

"Why was that?"

"Because her husband was not happy to see him. He punched Clay in the nose and knocked him into the bushes. Fortunately, the cab driver saw it happen, so Clay was able to ride back to Logan with him, which was also too bad."

"Why was that?"

"Because Clay went to the Delta lounge and had a bunch of drinks, which was again too bad."

"Why was that?"

"Because he missed the last shuttle flight back to New York, which was really too bad."

O'Brien was getting tired of this game. "And?"

"Because he went on a bender in Boston, eventually ended up back at the airport last night where he fell asleep and someone stole his shoes."

"You mean he's in Logan Airport without any shoes?"

"Not any more. He found a sneaker store, something to do with the Boston Celtics. He's taking the shuttle to New York, he should be in the air right now."

"Listen, Charlie, when you talk to him again, make sure to tell him to call me here at the agency. O.K.? As soon as he can."

"You got it, Dennis."

O'Brien hung up. "Damn it," he muttered to himself. One more screw up by Clay. The work hard, play hard routine was breaking down. The best account man in the agency was committing suicide. It had to be addressed.

He buzzed the intercom. "Evelyn, no matter where I am this morning find me if Clay Walker calls."

He sat back in the hammock again. The lawyer had called. Every time he called, O'Brien got sick to his stomach. The divorce proceedings made him feel out of his element, in an alien and punitive world. Now, there was this urgent call. He picked up the phone, called Sandy instead.

"Sandy, it's me, Dennis. We need to get together to talk about Global. For the next sixteen days that's going to be the only account on my mind. Yours too, I hope. What's happening? Have you seen any good things?"

"I'm looking at some ideas beginning in a half hour. The first stop is McCloskey's office."

"Good, I'll pick you up on my way over."

. . .

Sandy waited in the hallway as he approached. O'Brien felt elated to see her. The clothing she wore seemed consistent with her personality. She had on a summery outfit, a short white skirt that exaggerated her tan, muscular legs, a bright patterned blouse. Had she gotten the tan from being away at the beach with some man? He cleared his throat. "Why are we meeting in McCloskey's office, Sandy?"

"It's a trick I learned from you, Dennis. You told me if you meet in your own office it's hard to end the meeting. People don't leave. You're trapped. This way you can escape whenever you want."

"That's one I should remember more often myself. Here we are."

Like most of the agency's creative people, the decor and atmosphere of McCloskey's office reflected the personality of the occupant. The room was dark except for the light given off from a large neon light shaped to spell "McCloskey" which hung suspended in the middle of the room. Save for a small low table, which served as a desk, the furniture consisted of a half dozen cushions strewn about the floor. Sandy and Dennis dropped down into two of the seats. Several creative people that worked in McCloskey's group sat sporadically about the room on the remaining cushions.

As the head of the Global effort, Sandy knew it would be her responsibility to comment on the ideas presented, despite the presence of O'Brien. She knew from experience that O'Brien would only intercede if necessary. She reminded herself that her job was to react to ideas in a direct manner, rejecting those ideas which had no merit, making suggestions for improvement on those with potential, applauding any that might be out and out winners, a rare occurrence. Most of all she had to make criticism without offending the creative people themselves. These were individuals she had to work with day after day, project by project. There was little room for error in massaging these sensitive egos. No matter how bad the work was on any given day, there would be other days, other work. If she wanted to become creative director of the agency she had to earn their respect. She brushed her short cut hair away from her face and looked at McCloskey, the lone person standing in the office. "How are you guys coming along?"

There were a half dozen different campaign ideas, each represented by two or three storyboards. As McCloskey showed the work it was clear to Sandy that there was little to salvage.

"Tell me, Mac, why in this campaign do the pictures have little to do with the words? You show pictures of airline passengers, but the words are all about Global's network of cities. Can't you find a way to integrate the elements? Make the story more cohesive?"

"On this next campaign I don't find your argument succinct or to the point of the strategy. It rambles. You don't leave the viewer with one clear promise. You make points about the airline's sophisticated reservations system, the size of the fleet, the experience of the employees, the range of Global's geography, everything. But, there's no driving drama."

Sandy held up another storyboard. "This one strikes me as too derivative. I keep thinking I've seen it all too many times before. Smiling faces going places. In fact, it reminds me of the 'Global Pride' campaign. We don't want to go backwards. We need something more original, fresher."

She pointed to a storyboard which had been placed against the wall. "Where's the scope of the airline here? The idea of the chairman doing a stand-up is old hat. Plus," she looked at O'Brien, "it's not politically correct to show the old chairman of the agency when there is a young aggressive president newly arrived. We're trying to dramatize how big Global is, the size and breadth of its service. We need something with stature, something uplifting, something soaring."

There were no more ideas to comment on. "Well, it's unfortunate we haven't been given more time on this project. I realize all of you have other accounts to work on, but we've got to keep trying. I think Dennis agrees that all those accounts cease to exist between now and the day of our presentation." She looked over at O'Brien, who nodded in agreement. "Why don't we plan on getting together in two days, say Thursday morning at nine, to see where we're at?"

Sandy and O'Brien walked back toward his corner office. "What do you think, Dennis? It was disappointing, wasn't it?" She brushed her hair back.

O'Brien watched her hand. He loved her habit of pushing her hair back. For a second he wondered what it would feel like to run his hand through her hair. "The only quality in that meeting was in your comments, Sandy. Who's next on your list? I hope it's better. We're looking at the makings of a disaster." He eyed the phone call slips from Evelyn as he talked. The top one said, "Your lawyer called again. It's urgent, he has to talk to you about child custody." O'Brien disappeared into his office before Sandy had a chance to reply.

. . .

The Indianapolis Hilton

This was the kind of situation with Baxter that most bothered Fran. She dialed the hotel operator, got connected to the dining room. "Hello, this is Mrs. Irwin, I talked to you earlier. I'm looking for Mr. Baxter, he's having dinner there."

"He was here, but he left a while back."

She hung up. It was ridiculous. Before they left New York to come to Indianapolis Baxter knew that they would have to finalize the negotiation for the World Series buy. She was the NBC contact for Global, but he had the responsibility and the power to make the decision. Now, he was off somewhere, unreachable. He had to know she was looking for him, with all the messages she'd left. He enjoyed irking her. She called home.

"Larry, Hi, it's me."

"How's it going today? What's going on in sunny Indianapolis?"

"You've been watching the weather channel again. The only thing sunny in Indianapolis is the weather."

"What's the problem?"

"I told you about the World Series buy. NBC has added a new wrinkle, a good one, but there's a deadline for us to respond and I can't get hold of Baxter."

"If it's a good deal why don't you take it? Why do you need him?"

"He'd go crazy. I'd be overstepping my bounds. He's the media expert, which is true. But, this offer from NBC is a no-brainer."

"So, do it."

"It's not worth the chance. It's difficult enough working for him without going around him."

"Then, leave messages for him all over the hotel."

"I have. I've called everyplace. He's here somewhere. I keep missing him."

"Then, tape a note to his door. Hey, it's not your fault."

"It would be if something went wrong with the buy. But, I'll do that, leave a note on his door, it's the one thing I haven't done. I'll talk to you later."

She wrote two notes, one for the outside door, one she would slip under the door. She took the elevator to the top floor. One of his fixations was his room had to be on the top floor, part of his need to be important.

She went down the corridor looking for his room number, found it. To her relief the door was ajar. Good. He'd returned. She knocked and stepped in at the same time. "Maynard, it's Fran, are you here?"

The scene startled her. Later, back in her own room, she'd tried to picture it, but it was a blur. Two girls, nude, saw her and ran into the bedroom. Baxter stood with a St. Thomas condo owner, both in their underwear. There was a pile of cash on the table between them. The condo owner attempted to shove the money into a small drawer, a futile effort. Baxter gestured toward Fran with the drink in his hand.

"Fran, what are you doing here? Say hello to ... Look, Fran, maybe I should call you when I'm free."

She had turned and fled, actually running to the elevator, escaping, mortified and ashamed at what she had witnessed. Back in her room, she sat in a chair, trembling. She wanted to call Larry, but couldn't.

An hour later, Baxter had come to her room as though nothing had happened. They discussed the NBC situation, decided on a course of action. Then, subdued, almost apologetic, he talked to her about the need for secrecy. How there was no need to say anything, nothing to gain. After all, they were in it together, the implication being that Baxter would make sure that Fran was part of it, if it were to get out. Fran had listened silently, embarrassed, humiliated by the knowledge she would be unable to report what was going on. What did they call people like herself? An accessory to the fact? Then, Baxter talked about the agency vote coming up, as though that were part of their conspiracy, part of Baxter's hold on her. How it made sense to go along with Swenson if he wanted to dump the agency. If the two of them were smart (always them together), if they were smart they would go along. Didn't it make sense to please the man who was going to run the airline? Of course it did. Fran had remained silent and Baxter had accepted her reaction as tacit agreement and had left satisfied. Fran Irwin sat on the bed and vowed to get even with him.

• • •

DAY 15

San Sebastian

From where they sat Murphy could see the coastline stretching both north and south. It was steaming, in the high 80's, but the ocean wind was stiff, cooling. The salt was pungent in the air.

The lunch had been spectacular, heightened by the extra care and attention to detail the Minister inspired wherever he went on the island. Murphy felt an unusual sense of contentment, an ease derived from financial well being. He sipped on a Cuba libre and admired the girl from afar as she played in the surf.

"*Señor* Murphy, can I ask you a personal question?"

He was jarred from his reverie. "It wouldn't be the first one."

"No, I'm serious. I want to talk to you about something, a separate business possibility, a new venture, but first, tell me what you do with your extra money. I kid you about your gambling. I know you like the action. I hope you don't have a problem."

"I don't." He assumed a confident air. "In fact, I do quite well. Gambling's like anything else, you have to do your homework. You have to bet with your head, never your heart."

The Minister wiped his mouth with his napkin. "That's interesting. Good. The point is, a man's got to invest his money wisely, for the future." He waved the napkin in the air. "Most people, if they're lucky, have maybe five, ten years when their income is greater than their expenses, years when they have some good money left over. What they do with that money has a lot to do with their retirement, how well they live. You agree?"

"Absolutely."

"Well, my personal question is what do you do with your extra dollars? Let me get right to the point. I have an interesting opportunity you might want to consider, something you might want to participate in."

Murphy moved his chair closer to the table.

"As you know, I am familiar with most activities on the island. I try to keep an eye on things. It's part of my job, but it's part of my nature too. A man can't be too knowledgeable, you agree?"

"I would say that you seem to know anyone who's anybody on the island."

"Well, San Sebastian is my home and I like people."

Murphy waved at the waiter for another drink. There were no meetings that afternoon. He turned his chair directly toward the Minister.

"There are many investment opportunities on the island: condo's, hotels, that sort of thing. As tourism goes up, thanks to our efforts," he raised his glass to Murphy, "the island needs more rooms."

Murphy took off his sunglasses. "From the agency's projections the island should see double digit increases for the next few years, at least."

"No doubt. Which means that owning space can be a good thing."

"What kind of space?"

"Let me be specific. There is a new hundred unit condo complex being built just north of here, near Vista Bueno. It's on the cliff overlooking the beach. It's going to be something, believe me. If you're interested I'll show it to you." He took out a pen and started writing on the back of the menu. "The plan is to finance ninety percent of the deal. We're interested in maximum leverage, as little of our own money tied up as possible."

"Won't that mean a lot of interest costs?"

"Not really. You see, I have friends at the bank, actually my cousin, Pedro Hernandez. You've met him."

"Ah, yes, a smart man."

"The best. Anyway, to get to the point, he's willing to give us a ninety percent mortgage at three percent interest."

"Three percent? I never heard of such a low rate. In the States the mortgage rates now are more like eight percent."

"Well, that's the point. When you're dealing with friends you get special attention."

"Very special."

"For every dollar we put up the bank puts up nine. Like I said, maximum leverage."

"So you don't have much at risk."

"Exactly. But, here's the best part. We've run some numbers and it looks like," he drew on the menu, "like we would need an average occupancy rate of seventy percent, year-round, to break even."

"That sounds pretty high to me. There are some soft periods during the year."

"That's true. But, in our case we have some insurance, some protection against the downside."

"How's that?"

"Well," he looked around, pulled his chair closer to the table, beckoned Murphy to do the same, "what I have to say to you is of the utmost secrecy. Of course, everything we talk about is confidential. You know that. But, this is extra. Strictly between you and ... "

"You know you can trust me, Ramon. We've been partners for almost four years."

"True. And I do trust you." He reached over and squeezed Murphy's hand, looked up. "Isn't she beautiful?" Murphy turned around. The girl was jogging slowly up the beach, graceful, firm strides in the shallow water. The Minister didn't wait for a reply. "We have protection because we're going to sign a long term deal with Global Airlines."

Murphy jerked around, faced the Minister. "Global?"

"Global's big in the vacation business. Year-round packages. No one knows that better than you."

"Do I ever. It's big business. Not only for them. For Burns & Cody, too. A lot of advertising, plus brochures. Huge."

"Yes. In this case we've offered them an exclusive with the condo property. And they're signing on. Five years. Seventy units."

"You're saying that just with the Global deal you've got a guaranteed break-even."

"You've got it. I'll show you the financial sheets. Each point of occupancy over and above break-even, seventy percent, spills a million in cash profit to us. We figure we can get to at least eighty percent with the island's promotions, the stuff we do with Burns & Cody."

"That's incredible."

"I'll show you the numbers. You can figure on a forty percent return on your investment per year, plus a big capital gain when we sell the property in five years."

"Good God."

The Minister's teeth glinted in the sun. "I thought you'd like it. If you're interested we'll allow you one-hundred thousand of participation. What do you think?"

"What's the rub here?"

"I'm only doing it because you've been a good partner. Everything is going smoothly with our arrangement." He wiped his mouth again with the napkin. "And I like you. There's no rub." He stared after the girl. "One other thing on this. This should amuse you. The Global guy, Maynard Baxter, needed a little grease to make the deal."

"How much grease?"

"Fifty grand per year. He did pretty well. If he makes the same kind of bread on all his deals for Global he's a rich man."

Murphy stared at the Minister.

"Don't worry, Red, there's nothing to worry about. It's a cash deal and you're not involved. I just thought you'd be amused. You know him?"

"Know him? Everybody in the airline and media business knows him. He's one of my major clients. He's got one of the biggest jobs in the airline."

"Not big enough for him, I guess." The Minister leaned back, took out a cigar. "Let's have a little celebratory drink, eh? You and I. It's a beautiful day, right partner?"

Murphy sat back. "Say, Ramon, I was thinking. This condo project, maybe we could make an arrangement where I could rent one of the apartments, you know, to stay in. I'm here every week and checking in and out of hotels is a pain. If I had an apartment it would be easier. I could leave some clothes here. I could get the agency to pay for it, I'm sure. It would probably be cheaper than the hotels. What do you think?"

"I think it's an excellent idea. The first units at the condo are finished. Let's go take a look later. It makes sense. It's a good idea."

Murphy nodded, turned back toward the sea and the girl. He relaxed in his chair, slipped out of his shoes. He closed his eyes, tried to lapse into his earlier meditation. But, he was distracted. His mind was spinning.

. . .

Global Airlines

Swenson put his feet up on his desk, read the press release to himself.

> Global Airlines announced today that Philip Richardson will join its board effective immediately. Mr. Richardson will fill the vacancy left by Peter Ross, who retired in March of this year.
>
> Mr. Richardson, formerly a managing partner at Goldman Sachs, is head of the investment banking concern, Richardson & Richardson. He is a graduate of Harvard and the Harvard Business School, resides with his wife and two children in Hyannisport, MA.
>
> Besides bringing strong financial experience Mr. Richardson is ...

Swenson's buzzer rang.

"Mr. Swenson, Mr. Richardson is here for his 3:00 p.m. meeting. Shall I send him in?"

Swenson walked to the door of his office, opened it, greeted Richardson, "What's this I hear about you becoming a flyer? You should have talked to me first, Stan."

"I'm not a fighter pilot, Bill. The Cessna I have is a little tame for your tastes. But, I'm happy to report that I have soloed."

"What's going on, a new hobby?"

"No, this isn't a mid-life crises. It's pure practicality. In fact, I'm not that fond of flying, but it just made sense, considering where we live and the amount of traveling I do. This way, I can shoot down to LaGuardia or up to Logan in no time. It was a headache doing it commercially. Do you realize how few flights there are into and out of Hyannisport?"

"I know we're the only big airline with slots there. Anyway, you're a brave man. These days, I'm happy to sit in the back of the aircraft."

"Next time you come to Hyannis let me know and I'll come down and pick you up."

"It's a deal." Swenson pushed the button under his desk that released his door, closing it. "Now, Stan, let me tell you about the director's job. First of all, I'm delighted you've accepted. It'll be good to work with an old friend. And, your name brings an aura of credibility to the board. As you know, we've got big financial problems."

"I've been reading the reports you've been sending."

"It's a crucial time for the airline, not just financially, but across the board. Frankly, this airline's been acting like the world isn't changing, but you and I know it is and an airline, any company, has to be in a position to guide its destiny. It can't just react to outside events."

"It hasn't been a good period for Global. Is it worse than you thought it would be before you took the presidency?"

"Much worse. There was too much of a business-as-usual attitude around here. I've had to take some dramatic steps. And, I've only just started." Swenson stood up, went to the window, turned back to the other man. "The plain truth is I can't do a thing without a strong, supportive board."

"You can count on me."

"Great." He opened a file on the table. "This will explain the benefits of a directorship. Salary, thirty-five thousand, forty thousand options at the striking price determined by the date of your joining the board, which is tomorrow. Plus, there's a twenty-five thousand pension that goes along with it."

"That's generous."

"It is. We've had to provide strong incentives to attract the best people to the board ... because of our condition. And, of course, we have full D & O insurance to protect you against any law suits, class actions, that sort of activity."

"I appreciate that. Bill, it's an excellent turn-around situation. I'm sure that's the way you see it."

"I wouldn't be here if it wasn't. Stan, we've been working together since I joined Citibank, so you know how I think. I haven't changed, except I'm probably more impatient."

"You can't change a big company without radical thinking and action."

"Good. We're in synch. Now, if you have your calendar handy there are some meeting dates I want to give you. The first one is in a little over two weeks, June 14th, it's a Monday. It'll be your first board meeting. It begins at noon. But, before the board meeting, that morning, there is a meeting about advertising I would like you to attend."

"Advertising is not my forte."

"Nor mine, although I've learned a little about it. On the 14th, our agency, Burns & Cody, and most likely, one other agency will make presentations and I'd like you to be there."

"What in God's name for?"

"I need a board member to break an unlikely, but possible, tie vote."

"And you want me ... "

"I want you to cast the deciding vote if there is a tie."

"And?"

"Stan, I've made up my mind to change agencies. The Burns & Cody relationship, while a good one in many ways, represents the old guard around here, the old way of running an airline, the one that's failed."

"So, the agency is a symbol of the total picture."

"Exactly, and I want to change it. And, I may have to count on your vote to do that."

"I don't know a damn thing about advertising, but I hear what you're saying. I said before that I would be supportive of your position and I will be."

"It's for the good of the airline, believe me." He picked up the file. "Some of these papers need your signature, if you've got a few more minutes. And then I want to take you over to see Haps Corwin. He wants to welcome you to the board. I know the two of you go back a long way."

. . .

Burns & Cody

The three secretaries sat attentively across from Clay Walker's desk. "So, ladies, let me take you through the questionnaire. The first point is this. You absolutely must get through to the individuals assigned to you. I'll be giving each of you a list of executives to call. Make sure you talk to each of them directly.

"Now, the first statement is important to get their attention. You say, 'Mister or Ms. So-and-So, top management is conducting a survey of the agency's executives. The information gained from the survey will be used to guide management in the conduct of a special program. Your personal response will contribute to the agency's conclusions about this special program. Please be as open and candid as possible.'"

"Now," Clay went on, "pause after that first statement. Let it sink in. Some of the respondents might have a question or two. The important idea is to reassure them that the information will be analyzed for the sole use of making a general conclusion about the program.

"Once they understand the basic idea, you should get quickly into the questionnaire. If they get itchy explain to them the entire survey only takes five minutes.

"Now, let me read the questions. Then, if you'd like, we can talk about them. Here they are.

"One, do you enjoy being out in the wilderness? Is this something you have experience with? How would you feel about the opportunity to spend an entire week alone on the side of a mountain?

"Two. Do you have experience with fasting? Do you enjoy going without food and water for extended periods of time?

"Three. Many people love animals. Perhaps you're one of them. How do you feel about snakes? What about tarantulas? Do you have any specific feelings toward wolves? What about bears?

"Four. Do you own a rifle or pistol? What about a tent? Have you ever used a bolo knife?

"Five. Tell me which of the following shots you have received in the past six months. Diphtheria? Malaria? Lyme Disease?

"Finally, could we have the name of your next of kin?

"Ladies, that's it. Just a few short questions. Now, there is no need to write down any of their replies. Unless someone answers positively to any of the questions. If that happens I would like to know exactly who said exactly what. The last point is this. Today's Tuesday. This survey must be done by Friday. If someone's out of town tell their secretary that it is critical that they be reached because this is a very important management survey. Call people at home if necessary. Any questions?"

"Just one, please," said one of the girls. "How did you get that bump on your head?"

"Oh, that. I was hit by a baseball bat."

• • •

DAY 14

Fifth Avenue

There was a sense of foreboding about the agency in Murphy's mind. As the time shortened to the Global presentation, the account became paramount in people's thoughts. Whether one was directly involved or not, you knew that the loss of the business would have disastrous effects. Rumors spread of mass firings. As someone so closely identified with the account, Murphy was looked upon as an indicator of the agency's fortunes. Some asked him directly the state of the situation, others gave him a quizzical look or a hopeful glance, seeking reassurance.

Murphy pretended it would work out. "Just a review, no other agencies involved," he would tell them. Inwardly, he was terrified. It bothered him that he knew little more about it than the average employee. When he arrived at the agency he no longer felt the air of familiar friendliness that had built up over a career. He was uneasy, particularly in the presence of anyone from senior management. It appeared to him that they didn't want to look him straight in the eye. He decided more than ever to look for ways to further his position, to extend his financial stake through opportunistic means. He would press the idea of moving himself and the tourism account to another agency at his next meeting with Ramon. As he strode up Madison Avenue toward the Global building he checked his calendar again to confirm that he would be in San Sebastian in a few days.

He had no particular business agenda with Jack Kreeger this day. Murphy had contrived a reason for the meeting. He was acting as though each trip to Global could be his last one, that any minute he would be called to be told he was off the business, that there was something to take advantage of in some unknown way while he still had access to Global. For the past week he had sought a means for being alone in Kreeger's office, free to investigate his papers in an effort to learn something that could be useful. So far no opportunity had presented itself. Each time he and Kreeger had met, Kreeger had left his office only briefly to give some paper or some instruction to his secretary. Today, Kreeger had told him that he needed to leave at 5:00 pm in order to go home. That left Murphy with little time, less than an hour.

O'Brien was correct in his observation that Global treated their building like a vast aircraft and that each visitor should be examined accordingly, as a potential terrorist. The screening routine was familiar to Murphy, but aggravating. First, he had to sign in. Then, the security desk had to call the person he was visiting. Only then was he allowed through to the elevators.

Leaving the building was more difficult. A visitor could leave only if accompanied by an employee of the airline. The employee would show his ID card and the visitor would be allowed to go. The airline's employees left through a special turnstile that opened when the employee inserted his ID. The people at the security desk, like all small people entrusted with a modicum of authority, acted as if they were protecting state secrets.

Kreeger was alone in his office when Murphy arrived. He gave his usual effusive greeting, accompanied by a strong handshake that was painful if you were not prepared for it. Murphy wondered if Kreeger would act any differently on the day the agency was dismissed, if that came to pass. He was sure he would be the same.

"Jack, I'm glad you could see me on such short notice. I wanted to show you the proof of the Roanoke ad, it came out great." He placed the proof on Kreeger's desk, then took two sheets of paper from his coat pocket, handing one to Kreeger, who studied it. "This is the latest status report. The agency's on track on all of these, Jack. The big project, other than our on-notice presentation, is the campaign for next winter. I wanted to confirm the date for the meeting as Thursday at 10:00 and to find out who'd be there from the airline."

"Just Ted Crowther and myself. Ted called me today as a matter of fact, he wanted to check the time of the meeting, so I know he'll be there. Say, Malachy, would you like some coffee or something?"

"I could use a Coke. Thanks."

"Let me tell Vera. I'll be right back. This coffee runs right through me. I should cut down."

Kreeger stepped out of the office and spoke to his secretary. Then, there was silence. Murphy stood up and looked out at the secretarial area. He could see the girl disappearing around the corner, heading for the refreshment area down the hall. He stepped behind Kreeger's desk, tried the various drawers. All locked. He went through the few papers on his desk. Nothing interesting. He stood and looked about the office, disappointed. Kreeger's coat hung on a hanger behind the office door. Murphy patted the coat, found a large wallet in the right hand pocket. There were several compartments in addition to the main opening for the paper money. He zipped open the largest compartment, exposing a packet of credit cards. Half way through the pile he found Kreeger's ID card. He put it in his pocket, returned the rest of the cards to the wallet. He had just sat down when Kreeger returned, the secretary following with the Coke.

"What else, Malachy? You know I've got to leave. My daughter's in a school play."

"That's about it, Jack. Take the status report with you. If you have any questions, call me."

Kreeger busied himself with some last minute instructions to his secretary, prepared to leave.

"Say, Jack, do you mind if I use your phone to call the agency? Vera can let me out. I won't be long." He smiled at Vera.

"No problem, Malachy." He shook his hand again. "I'll see you soon."

Kreeger was gone. Murphy sat by the desk, the phone in his hand. In a few minutes Kreeger would be back, unable to leave the building without his ID. There would be a search, but hopefully not for long if Kreeger wanted to make his train. His secretary would have to let him out. Once he was gone, Murphy would have to figure a way to stay behind, to get rid of the girl. He held the phone to his ear and waited.

He could hear Kreeger's voice long before his return. He was calling his secretary as he sped down the hallway. He was out of breath when he entered the office, the girl behind him.

"I'll have to call you back," said Murphy to the phone. "Jack, what's going on?"

"I can't find my ID." The three of them began looking around the office for the missing card. Murphy got down on his knees. He looked up at Kreeger. "When was the last time you saw it?"

"This morning when I got here, I think. And at lunch, I imagine. Let's see, Mary Carey and I went out to lunch."

"Maybe that's it, Jack. You could have left it in the restaurant. And come back in the building on Mary's card."

"That could be it." He seemed satisfied for the moment. "Look, Vera, you'll have to let me out, we'll find it tomorrow. Call the restaurant. I'm late, I've got to make that train." He grabbed her arm, led her from the office.

Murphy sat down, his hand in his pocket, clutching the card. The secretary would be back in no time and she would be in a hurry to leave too, now that her boss was gone. He had no excuse to delay. He needed a ruse of some kind. Already he could hear someone approaching.

"Mr. Murphy, if you're finished calling the agency I can let you out."

"That's OK, Vera. I just learned I have to go to a meeting down in the media department. They can let me out. Thanks." He walked toward the elevator bank, but kept going. He cut back down a corridor, found a supply room. It was late, an unlikely time for anyone to be seeking supplies. He went in, found the light, shut the door. He would wait an hour or so and then check out the floor to see if anyone was around.

The room was jammed with materials, including copies of annual reports. The agency's chairman was always chiding them to read the annual reports of their clients. He could hear him. "You never know what you might learn that could be useful." Murphy sat on the floor behind the last row of shelves, in case someone entered unexpectedly. He had plenty of time to follow Brad Burns' advice.

. . .

Uncomfortable, he woke up, his back sore from the hard floor. It was already 6:30 p.m. Time to move. He opened the door to a strange silence, until he realized the familiar music from the intercom was off. Slowly, then faster, he traversed the short distance to Kreeger's office. The door was shut and locked. He ran his hand under the secretary's desk, hurt his finger on the nail that held the keys.

The door to Kreeger's office opened on the first try. He went in, shut the door behind him, turned on the light, breathed deeply, sat down in Kreeger's chair. He ran his hand under the desk, found a lone key on a nail. He turned the key in the center lock, heard a sequence of locks clicking as the drawers of the desk opened, one by one.

The center drawer contained a loose assortment of pencils, paper clips, some business cards. Nothing of any value. The large drawer on the right side of the desk slid open easily, revealing a dozen or so neatly arranged file folders. Murphy examined the files, which were in alphabetical order. "Agency" was first.

The folder contained a number of production estimates for ads yet to be produced, some recent status reports, a few storyboards, a half dozen memos. Murphy examined the memos deliberately. The last one, a note from Kreeger's assistant, Mary Carey, caused him to lean forward, his mouth open. He reread the letter, which was dated the previous day. The subject was "Second Agency" and said,

> For our forthcoming meeting with Mr. Swenson on this subject I have analyzed the top twenty-five agencies and narrowed the list down to five, based on the criteria we discussed with Mr. Swenson. Of the five listed below, one agency, Comnet, stands out. They have the size, reputation, financial strength, management, and related travel experience we seek. While they do not have a U.S. airline account they do have a number of regional airlines around the world. This experience would be useful as Global increases its worldwide presence. Please let me know if you need any more information. Otherwise, we will present these findings to Mr. Swenson at our meeting on Monday.

For the third time Murphy read the memo. Monday was just four days away. It was the day he would be in San Sebastian. There wasn't much time for him to act if he was going to put this information to good use. A vague idea of a plan came to him, but he pushed it out of his mind for the time being as he went back to the files. "Contracts," "Employee Benefits."

The next folder was "Financial Ads." The first letter was from Swenson to Kreeger. It, too, was dated the day before. It read,

> Because of the condition of the money markets, and especially Global's weak financial situation, it may occur periodically that we will have to run an ad or two addressed to our various constituencies, such as the unions or our stockholders. I would like to meet with you as soon as possible to discuss this highly confidential subject. I must emphasize that anything we do in this area will be of the highest secrecy. Any ads that run will be produced in-house, using an all-type format, with the intent of keeping the list of those aware of the ads to an absolute minimum.

Murphy gasped at the next memo. It was also from Swenson, dated that very day. It had an envelope attached with the wording, "This letter to be opened and read by the addressee only" in large block letters across the face. It read,

> As anticipated, we may soon have the need to run an ad because of the occurrence of an unusual financial event. We have been informed by one of our investment bankers that American Airlines is preparing a tender offer in the neighborhood of $25 per share for Global. This would be treated by Global as an unfriendly takeover, one we would resist despite the apparent near term advantage of such an offer to our stockholders. Please be in my office at 3:00 p.m. today to discuss this and be advised that this information is not to be shared with anyone under any circumstance.

Murphy leaned back, rubbed the back of his neck, rolled his head in a circular motion. "Holy shit," he said, louder than he should have. He got up, peeked out from the office. No one was in sight. Back at the desk, he continued his study of the remaining files. There was nothing further of use. But, he had uncovered not one, but two blockbuster pieces of information. It took him a few more minutes to finish his investigation of the remaining drawers. Most of the material was personal, pictures of Kreeger and his family, one of Swenson smiling, shaking hands with Haps Corwin, the airline's chairman. "Bullshit," said Murphy.

There was no one around on the floor or in the elevator to the lobby of the building. He slipped the ID card into the turnstile in a casual way, stepped through, then circled completely around the lobby. A lone Global security guard stood against a wall next to the entrance of the building's shopping arcade. Murphy handed Kreeger's card to the guard, "I found this on the sidewalk just outside, one of the employees must have dropped it by mistake." By the time the man had examined the card and looked up, Murphy was gone.

• • •

DAY 13

Burns & Cody

Murphy stood up, walked around Steve Swallow's office, lit a cigarette.

"Since when have you been smoking?"

"Since when have you been an outdoorsman? Nice boots." He picked up one slowly, exaggerating its weight.

"I hate the outdoors, but I've got to go to Outward Bound. I've tried every excuse, but the chairman's adamant. Which group are you in?"

"I'm not, that is, I haven't been notified. Except for a wacky phone survey I had to answer. I'm worried."

"You're paranoid, Murphy. The list hasn't been finalized."

"You call it paranoid to be running the biggest account in the agency when it's about to blow out the door?"

"Since when? You keep telling people not to worry. I've heard you."

"Well, I lie. You probably know more about what's going on then I do. You spend a lot of time with the chairman."

"When I'm with the chairman I'm the chief financial officer and that's it. We talk numbers. I rarely hear anything about the advertising business. Although I did overhear part of a conversation between him and Dennis O'Brien."

"And ... ?"

"They were talking about the Global presentation and who should be there. I didn't hear your name, but I also didn't hear the whole conversation."

"And you call me paranoid. I've got every reason to be uptight. What happens if they take me off the account? Do you know what that means? I'm fifty."

"You'd still have the tourism business."

"You're the head bean counter. You know damn well the agency can't afford me on just that account."

"Look, don't jump to conclusions. You have the reputation of being an A-1 account man. It's not your fault the airline's in review. Everyone knows that Swenson started this."

"Started it and will finish it."

"What do you know that I don't know?"

"Nothing." Murphy sat down, put the cigarette out.

"I've never seen you smoke."

"I've smoked since I was fourteen."

"I've known you a long time. I've never seen you with a cigarette."

Murphy dismissed him with a wave of his hand, sat down. "Look, I've got big news. This could be tremendous."

Swallow stared at him. "Don't tell me the Minister's at it again."

"No, but I see him Monday night. This is different and it's big. Last night, in Kreeger's office at Global, I saw a memo that blew my mind. It said that American Airlines was going to make a tender offer of $25 for Global." Swallow reached for the *Wall*

Street Journal on his desk. "Don't bother. I can tell you, Global closed at 12 yesterday."

Swallow cleared his throat. "Tell me about this memo."

"It's legit. It was from Swenson and it said they had information from one of their investment bankers that this offer was in the works."

"This is big. If it happened, that is. And, if you acted in time."

"You could double your money fast."

"Double? Double nothing. You could make ten times your investment."

Murphy stood up again. "How's that? If the stock's 12 and the offer's 25, that's double, isn't it?'

Swallow picked up his calculator. "Not if you buy some calls."

"Calls, you mean options?"

"Exactly." He punched at the calculator with his pencil. He opened the newspaper and scanned the financial pages. "Here it is." He worked his calculator again. "If you bought call options and the tender happened at 25 you'd make more than ten times your investment."

Murphy rubbed the back of his hand across his mouth. "My God, each hundred large bet would get you a mil."

"Bet is the right term."

"How's that?"

"Because if the stock doesn't go up during the life of the option you lose all your money. Every penny."

"How long?"

"In this case you'd probably want to buy a ninety day call."

"Is that what you're thinking of doing?"

"Not me. One letter does not make a deal."

Murphy leaned against Swallow's desk. "You're the perfect CFO, always careful. Afraid to risk your dough 'cause it's not a sure thing. To me this is an incredible piece of good fortune and I'm going to take advantage of it."

"Go ahead, it's your money. But, let me tell you about another risk. The government."

"The IRS?"

"No, the SEC. They look for unusual activity when something like this happens. Depending on how many options you buy they might want to talk to you. They might think it more than a coincidence that the agency guy on the Global account just happened to buy a bunch of options right before the stock jumped. So, you might be cautious."

"What's cautious?"

"Unless you have a history of buying options in big amounts anything might rouse their suspicions. Or, then again, they might not pick it up. It's up to you on the risk you want to take."

Murphy sat, silent. He toyed with the boot, snapping and unsnapping its big buckles. "On that conversation of the chairman's that you overheard, whose names did they mention?"

"Well, like I said I didn't hear everything, but it sounded like O'Brien and Sandy Stein, and they mentioned Clay Walker."

"Jesus Christ!" Murphy jumped up. "Clay Walker! He's an account guy. Don't you see? He'd be a logical choice if they were going to replace me on the account. Why didn't you tell me this earlier?"

"I guess I didn't make the connection."

Murphy fumbled with another cigarette. "Tell me exactly what they said about Walker."

"I can't remember. I just know his name came up. It may not even have been in the context of Global for all I know. I don't remember."

"Shit! Paranoid. I'm not paranoid. Not me." He lit the cigarette, got up to leave.

"For a guy who smokes you probably know you can't smoke in any of the common areas of the building."

"Yeah, yeah." He snuffed the cigarette out in Swallow's empty coffee cup. "Look, I'll see you after I get back from San Sebastian. I've got to run. I've got a lot to do in a hurry." He opened the office door.

"I'm sure you do," said Swallow. "Like call your broker."

Murphy went down the back stairway to his floor. Like call my broker. You bet your sweet ass I'm going to call my broker. This is no NBA game. This is a bet that has to be made. Big. Like a quarter million. That would win him two-and-a-half million. With that in the bank he wouldn't have to worry, ever.

He whistled to himself. This was turning into the biggest month of his life. He was part owner in a can't-miss condo complex in San Sebastian. He had the chance to move the tourism account to another agency. And, he could cash in big on the information about the second Global agency. He had mulled his plan for the second agency over in his mind a half dozen times. It was flawless.

. . .

O'Brien removed the top card from his office display, revealing the number 12. He tossed the card with 13 on it into his waste paper basket. "There were a few ideas for commercials that might be useful, don't you think?"

Sandy stared at the 12. "I liked the small airport spot. Dramatizing the big scope of the airline by showing one of the smallest destinations is a clever idea. It will be visually surprising."

"What about the eye-of-the-camera technique?"

"I like that approach for the second spot, the vacation commercial. It also lends itself to the short production schedule we have."

O'Brien watched her brush her hair back. "You could actually edit the commercial as you shot it on tape."

"I would use a hand held camera."

"I think that spot should be personally supervised by you, Sandy. The plan is to produce it in Bermuda." O'Brien sat down, threw up his hands. "But, we still need a theme, a line to wrap all this work under. You can't have a campaign without one."

"That's your area, Dennis, you're the wordsmith."

"We have over a dozen writers working on nothing else but theme lines, and that's just the New York office."

"Another missing element is the music."

"I received these tapes this afternoon, Sandy. If you'd like to hear them you're welcome. It's late I know. You probably have some plans."

"Thanks, I'd like to hear them. If you can give me ten minutes I'll be right back."

O'Brien followed her out of his office, picked up a pile of mail Evelyn had prepared. There was a note on top.

> I put a corned beef sandwich in your refrigerator
> in case you get hungry. You have to eat once
> in a while. See you tomorrow.
> Evelyn.

He went back into his office. The music tapes were piled by his cassette player. Sandy would be there in a minute. He began to straighten his office. The room seemed too bright. He lowered the dimmer on the wall.

Sandy knocked on the door, walked in. "How many tapes have come in?"

"This is everything. Two New York houses, plus one each from L.A. and Nashville. I'll put the first one on. Each of these themes is demonstrated in the four styles we requested: jazz, country, rock and contemporary. We wanted to be sure the music had versatility."

They sat in silence, listened to the music.

"This one may be versatile, but there's nothing exciting about the basic music, do you think?"

"Let's try the Nashville tape."

Simultaneously, they reached for the pile of tapes, knocking several on the floor. As they knelt to retrieve them, O'Brien lost his balance, fell against Sandy, her head brushing against his chest. He braced himself from falling further by grabbing her shoulder. She fell against him, her hair brushing his face, soft against his cheek. How often had he wondered what her hair felt like? He reached for the back of her neck, clasped her hair in his hand, pulled her toward him. He swallowed several quick breaths, inhaled the clean scent from her shampoo. Holding her with both hands, he raised himself up, pulled her with him, against him. He kissed her hair, then her forehead, took a step back. She looked at him, confused, but willing. He put his arms around her, kissed her lightly on the mouth. He was unprepared for the way he felt, the impact of her body against him, all his senses sharp to sensations long neglected. Had he ever felt like this? His kisses became bolder; against her neck, her ears, her mouth. He tightened his arms around her body.

O'Brien took her hand, guided her toward the hammock. Sandy looked about, stopped, caught her breath. "Dennis, this is all happening too fast." She turned toward the door. "Excuse me, I ..." She walked from his office, running her fingers through her hair.

He watched her go, collapsed into the hammock, stared across the room out the window into the darkness. He sat there for five minutes, collected his thoughts, picked up his phone and dialed. "Can we talk? ... I understand. I'm sorry. Of course, not tonight. I didn't plan it, it just happened ... Maybe, we could have a drink. I've got to talk to you ... Everything you're saying makes sense. But, I can't change the way I feel. Will you have a drink with me? Good, I'll meet you at the Oak Room at the Plaza after the Global copy meeting."

. . .

Grand Central Station

The chill against his feet woke Clay. He pulled his coat jacket close around his neck. He was aware that his back ached. The early stages of a hangover were setting in. The combination of the cold and the pain, the early morning light and noises, would deny him more sleep. He opened his eyes partially to the eerie scene, almost church-like except for the smells. The light was beginning to seep in through the windows high above. The mammoth room was coming alive to the initial stages of the commuter scene: a few briefcase carriers, some lunchbox carriers, a man with a dolly loaded with newspapers, a couple of bums yawning nearby.

He eased himself up from the hard bench, his back more painful now. His feet hit the stone floor, the sudden cold jolting him with the idea that his shoes had been stolen. Again, he thought. His close friends at the agency, the few that helped him in these situations, had recently started calling him Clay No-shoes and Clay New-shoes. Twice in the last few months, on short notice, they had gone to Brooks Brothers to get him a new pair of 10½ medium, brown cordovans.

He stretched, turned around. The big clock in the center of the room told him he couldn't depend on his friends today. But, at 6:00 a.m. he had no intention of going home either.

He walked directly across the huge expanse toward the Vanderbilt Avenue exit. He remembered Yogi giving him the clenched fist signal, no more pitches tonight. He had tried a few unsuccessful phone calls to a former girlfriend in Westhampton. He had walked from P.J.'s to Grand Central, but must have fallen asleep waiting for the last train. With relief he reached down and felt the wad of bills at the bottom of his front pants pocket, the place he'd taken to carrying his cash since his wallet had been stolen.

There was a bar he knew across the street on Vanderbilt that he thought opened early. He would hide out there until he could get some help, until the stores opened. He never drank during the day, but today he would have a Bloody Mary for medicinal purposes.

• • •

DAY 10

Burns & Cody

Murphy shut his office door behind him. His worst weekend fears were confirmed. He kicked his desk hard, recoiled from the stab of pain. He picked up a pile of magazines from his table and hurled them about the room, screamed, "Fuck!"

His intercom buzzed. "Mr. Murphy, are you O.K.?"

"No. In fact, it couldn't be worse. But, there's nothing you can do to help, I'm afraid. Hold all calls."

He sat down at his desk, head in his hands. How could they do this to him? After all he'd done for the agency. The chairman had said taking him off the account had nothing to do with his performance, that he had done a fine job on Global, that it had been a showcase account for the agency and a giant profit maker.

That it wasn't Murphy's fault that Swenson had appeared on the scene, was shaking things up. The agency needed to show a renewed enthusiasm for the business and putting new faces on would help. They had introduced Sandy Stein in creative and they would now bring in Clay Walker as the top account man. Clay Walker. Didn't the chairman know he was a drunk? How the hell could he handle the biggest account?

And then the chairman had lied to him, telling him there'd be other accounts for him to handle, that as soon as the Global problem was past they would reallocate the accounts in the agency, giving Murphy something besides tourism to run. He didn't believe the chairman. He was the only one in the agency who knew the truth about Global, that a second agency was in the works, that the presentation was a formality, a charade being staged by Swenson. When the account was gone the agency would take a financial bath. Murphy would become part of the mass exodus that would ensue.

He looked at his watch. He had twenty minutes to get to Comnet. And then he would go straight to the airport for his trip to San Sebastian. He unlocked his closet, took out the briefcase and unlocked it. There was one packet of bills remaining, a few thousand dollars. He still couldn't accept the fact about how much he had lost betting. None of his recent bets had paid off. He would have to dip into his savings, but only briefly. The Global tender offer payoff would happen any day and then he would be rich. Add to that the moving of the tourism account to a new agency plus the deal he was about to make with Comnet and he would be extremely rich. If everything went according to plan he would have it made for life. He closed the case, checked his watch again. He would have to hurry.

. . .

666 Fifth Avenue

Murphy scanned the lobby directory until he found it, "Comnet Worldwide Headquarters - 55th floor."

As he stepped off the elevator a huge panoramic three dimensional map of the world was displayed along the opposite wall under the Comnet company logo. Colored lights representing office locations emblazoned the maps. There was a color code: blue for public relations, green for direct marketing, white for medical, red for advertising. The effect was dazzling.

"Do you like our little display?" Murphy recognized Spiro Bates from the many pictures he had seen of him in the trade news. Bates was smiling, pleased by Murphy's absorption in the graphic. How many times had Bates, hidden from view, watched visitors take in the effect. The man looked even fatter and more dishevelled than in his pictures. "Mr. Murphy, it's good to meet you. Come on back to my office."

"It's good of you to meet with me on such short notice."

"From what you said on the phone I would have met you any place at any time. It sounds very exciting. I'd like to hear more about it. But, first tell me about yourself." He offered Murphy a cigar from a large humidor on the huge table at which they sat.

"No thanks, I'll just have one of these." Bates held out a lit match for Murphy to light his cigarette, then lit his cigar. "My career is a one-agency one, which I guess is unusual these days. I've always been an account man, worked on every kind of business you can imagine. For the past five years I've run the Global account, plus our tourism business, San Sebastian."

"I'm familiar with your Burns & Cody's work on both accounts, of course, it's won a stack of awards. Between you and me I've chided our people to equal it. And, both those accounts of yours are big pieces of business."

"That's true. Global spends one-hundred million and Tourism is about fifteen. And I can assure you they're both money makers. But, I'm here to talk about Global, although it's possible we might want to talk about Tourism some time."

"I'm intrigued. Tell me more."

"Well, no one knows what I'm about to tell you, but we're on thirty days notice on Global. In fact, we've got about ten days before we have to make a major presentation. But, the presentation, I can tell you, is just for show. Global's made up its mind to move the account to another agency."

"You don't say." Big puffs of aromatic smoke from the cigar engulfed the two men.

"There's a new airline president, Bill Swenson, who's shaking things up big time. He's ... "

"I know him, or rather I've seen him. He spoke at a Harvard Business School meeting I went to a couple of weeks ago. Brilliant."

"He's smart all right. And he's ambitious. He won't be happy until he's chairman of the airline. The current chairman, Haps Corwin, loves the agency, but with all the money problems Swenson's getting more say because of his financial expertise. Anyway, he's been shaking things up, putting what he calls his suppliers through some drills."

"And the agency's another supplier?"

"Exactly. They've set up a panel of voters, six of them, with a board member to act as a tie-breaker if the votes split, which is not about to happen."

"You know the voters, know where they stand?"

"I do, and as far as I can tell, the only sure votes for us are the chairman and his buddy, the marketing director, Ted Crowther. The rest of the characters, I'm certain, will go along with Swenson."

"So where does Comnet come in?"

"I happen to have a lot of close friends at Global."

"A good account man always does."

"Yes, and I know some things no one else does."

"Like?"

"Like they're deciding which agency they would like to invite besides us to make an agency presentation."

"You're saying only one other agency will be invited."

"That's right. Swenson's decided that. Just one agency to ..."

"Are you telling me that your agency is out and that there's only one agency being invited to present? That sounds like the second agency will get the business."

Murphy leaned forward. "You've figured it right."

"So how does one get invited to the party, Mr. Murphy?"

"Call me Malachy, or call me Red if you'd like."

"O.K., Red, how does Comnet get to make a presentation?"

"Well, it so happens that I'm involved in the selection process and that I can assure your agency of being invited to make a pitch if you're smart."

Bates leaned back, puffing hard. He spoke in a low deep voice, almost a whisper. "Tell me how I can be smart."

"It's very simple." Murphy took some papers from his coat pocket, gave one to Spiro Bates. "These numbers show the size and profitability of the Global account for the last three years. As you can see, we've been averaging four to five million dollars in profits."

Bates put his cigar down, held the sheet in both hands, examining it like it was a valuable diamond. "These numbers are extraordinary."

"It's not every day you can have a glamour account, do award-winning advertising and make a fortune in the process."

"I'm overwhelmed. How does Comnet participate?"

"Like I said, I'm involved, I have a lot of friends at the airline."

"Are you saying that you could insure Comnet's being invited?"

"That's correct."

"So, what's the deal?"

"That's a good word. Deal." He stood up. "I propose a simple one. First, you hire me to run the account. That makes business sense. I know the Global company inside and out and they like me. Having me here would make for a smooth transition between agencies. Who could argue with that?"

"Not me, I can assure you." He smiled at Murphy, bit down on his cigar, puffing to keep it lit. "But, I imagine there's more to the deal."

"All you have to do is pay me a million dollars the day you win the account, and a million dollars a year, guaranteed for five years. It's a small price to pay for such a prize account. I imagine the Comnet stock will jump enough on the good news of getting Global that it will pay for me at the start."

"That's a lot of money, Mr. Murphy. What if I said 'No'?"

"All I can tell you, Mr. Bates, is that there are a lot of agencies out there that would kill for the Global account. I'm sure one of them would be interested in my offer." Murphy stood up, started to leave.

"Just a minute, Red. Sit down. I think we might be able to make a deal. I admire a guy who knows how to strike a hard bargain. What you're saying is: if Comnet gets the business, you get yourself a job and a pile of money. If we don't get the account, we just forget about it. What's next?"

"I would like a contract, of course. But, a handshake will put things in motion. If we agree, you will be hearing shortly from Global. If I were you I would start preparing for a presentation immediately. By the way, that's something I could help you with."

Bates stood up. "I'll have a lawyer draw up the papers." He stuck out his hand to Murphy who grabbed it. Murphy resisted an urge to put both hands on Bates' hand. "I think I'm going to enjoy working with you, Red."

Murphy stepped toward the door. "I can find my way out. I'll call you in a day or so and we can meet to sign the contract. I'm heading to San Sebastian. I'll call you when I return." He retraced his steps to the elevator. Out of sight from Spiro Bates, he began slapping his hands together. This good fortune was beyond his hopes. A five million dollar arrangement. Add that to the couple of million he would make from the tender offer by American Airlines, plus whatever he could make by moving the Tourism account. The first thing he would do was buy the summer house his wife had always dreamed of having. He would do it as a surprise.

. . .

Spiro Bates picked up his phone. "Miss Blakely, did you get all that? Good, I want a complete transcript as soon as possible. Next, there are a number of people I want you to get hold of. I'm making a list of them for you. I want them here tomorrow at 7:00 a.m., no excuses. Come on in." He sat on his couch, twirling a new Havana in his mouth prior to lighting it. The first move was to make a run at Global before they called him. It had to look like Comnet was the pursuer. He would call Swenson, use Swenson's Harvard speech as a reason to see him. Play to his ego. The critical issue was to steal the account before other agencies learned of a possible switch by Global. Once the account was won he would take care of Murphy, the double crossing bastard. Who did Murphy think he was dealing with? He'd find out that he couldn't play games with Spiro Bates.

. . .

Global Airlines

Maynard Baxter took Kreeger aside. "Jack, what's the meeting all about? Do you know?"

"I don't know any more than Swenson's memo about having a staff meeting."

"On marketing matters."

"Right, Maynard."

"Will he ... ?"

"Good morning, gentlemen." Swenson burst into the conference room like a general into a command post. To Baxter he was the essence of the take-charge executive.

"We haven't gotten together since our first meeting a couple of weeks ago, so I thought it would be useful to update you. First of all, I want to reassure you that the financial state of the airline is not as dire as the press would make out. We will survive and grow, I can tell you. You should pass that on to the people that work for you. It's very unsettling for people to be worried about their jobs."

"Second, I want to talk about our situation with the agency. The presentation, which as voters you must plan on attending, is in ten days. We're holding the meeting in a room at LaGuardia as a convenience to our board members who will be in New York for a board meeting that afternoon. You should know that a second agency, Comnet, has been asked to make a presentation as a basis of comparison for us. Jack Kreeger's group analyzed the agencies available and recommended Comnet. By the way, Jack, Spiro Bates, the chairman of Comnet, called me before I had a chance to call him. He must have a keen ESP, don't you think?"

Kreeger smiled. "That's amazing. I ... "

"After the two agencies make their presentation that morning, we'll take our vote immediately on whether to hire Comnet or stand pat. I've asked Jack to provide you with the background material on Comnet in case you're not familiar with them. Any questions? ... Mr. Baxter?"

"I'm very familiar with Comnet. They have an outstanding media operation, best in the business, and they're strong worldwide."

"Yes, the overseas network they have is impressive. Anything else? Good. Jack, please come with me, I want to talk to you about that financial ad."

Baxter was left alone with Fran Irwin in the large room. "Well, Fran, that does it."

"Does what?'

"Don't you see? It's a set up. He's brought in Comnet for the kill. You better be ready to go with the flow."

"Just because he's got a second agency presenting doesn't mean he's going to change."

"Are you kidding? How come we have a new accounting firm, two new investment houses, even a new mergers and acquisitions law firm?"

"True."

"The guy's a mover, he's here to stay, and he's going to be chairman, it's just a matter of time."

"That doesn't mean I have to vote against the agency. It would be totally unjust."

Baxter stuck his head forward. "Unjust. What the fuck does justice have to do with it? This is about business and power. I'll wash your hand and you wash mine. That little presentation by Swenson was his way of telling us who the new agency was going to be, and that he was expecting our votes. That is, if we want to be part of his team."

"You certainly couldn't wait to praise Comnet."

Baxter laughed. "I was just saying, 'You can count on me, Boss.' Which is funny, because the other day I told Dennis O'Brien not to worry."

Fran Irwin stared at her hands.

"Don't give me the solemn routine. You better get with the program, if you like your job, which I happen to know you damn well do. C'mon, let's get out of here. It's never smart to hang around the executive floor looking idle." He walked from the room, looked back to make sure she was following.

. . .

P.J.'s

O'Brien eased himself into the booth across from Clay Walker. "What's the matter, are you sick?"

"I've been better." As if on cue, he sneezed twice, blew his nose. He looked at O'Brien. "How sickness enlarges the dimensions of a man's self to himself."

"That's Shakespeare. Probably Hamlet, right?

"Charles Lamb."

"I give up. Anyway, what do you have?"

"I don't know, early summer flu I imagine."

"Here's your ginger ale, Mr. Walker. Would you like a beer, Mr. O'Brien?"

"That would be fine, thanks." He watched the girl head for the bar. "Ginger ale, this is a first. You must be very sick."

"I'm having trouble eating and drinking."

"Maybe you should go home."

"There's too much work to do."

"Just the subject I was going to bring up."

"Work?"

"Yes, I was with the chairman today and it was decided to replace Murphy on Global."

"Really? I always thought he got the job done. That account must be a bitch."

"He did and it is. But, part of our plan to keep the business is to show a whole new team."

"Does Murphy know? I haven't seen him around the last few days. What happens to him?"

"The chairman talked to him, told him he'd be given something else to handle besides Tourism, once the Global situation is past. He's a good account man. I'm sure there'll be plenty for him to do. Anyway, the chairman and I talked about who might replace him and your name came up."

Walker coughed, then sneezed, got out his handkerchief.

"The chairman said he'd heard you were burning the candle too brightly at both ends, said he was concerned."

"What did he say?"

"Look, Clay, don't you realize you can't do the stuff you've been doing without the whole building talking about it? Chicago, Boston, these make for good stories, and agency types love good stories, especially when they're about someone they know. Plus, like everyone else, you have your enemies. The chairman thinks you're the best account man in the place, but he's worried about you. He was very reluctant to put you on our most important account at its most critical moment."

"Was?"

"I told him you were the best choice, that you would get your act together."

"How far out on the limb did you have to go?"

"I told you, he's high on you. He just needed reassurance."

"I'm grateful, it's a crucial position, the biggest one I've ever had. I think you're understating how far you had to go. The future of the agency hangs on the next few days. Which is true, isn't the presentation soon? What the hell can I do at this stage?"

"It's true we're out of time, behind the eight ball with ten days to go. We've got a smattering of good ads, stuff we polished over the weekend, but no unifying campaign theme, if you can imagine. The whole damn creative department is on the case now. But, there are things for you to do. I want you to jump into it head first, forget your other stuff, tell them you're sick. You don't have to make up a phony sick voice, you already have that. First, I want you to oversee one of our shoots. We'll probably make three commercials. There's one that particularly suits your experience. Then, there's the presentation itself, a chance for you to show your unique dramatic talents, and I'm not kidding, we need to put on a show."

"Can I ask you a question? What are our chances?"

"They're damn good. The chairman and I went through it again today. We know both the airline's chairman and marketing director are on our side. That's two sure votes. The other day Maynard Baxter, their media guru, told me personally he was in our corner. Fran Irwin, who works for Baxter, is not going to go against her boss. That's two more votes, or four of the total of six."

"Who are the other two voters? Swenson and ... "

"Jack Kreeger, the advertising director. He's in Swenson's pocket. But, you know, the funny thing is I think we impressed Swenson when he was at the agency. It's possible all six votes will go for us."

"What's the story on other agencies getting into this?"

"That's the most encouraging part, there's no other agency in this, so it's unlikely they would be making a change."

"That is encouraging. Getting back to the vote, tell me what happens if it splits three to three."

"Apparently, one of the board members will be there to break any tie."

"Who is he?"

"A guy named Richardson. We don't know a lot about him, except the chairman of the airline says he has no axe to grind. He thinks he's more likely to stay with us, the status quo, then shake things up. He's a banker. Anyway, nobody sees a split vote."

"I want you to know I'm appreciative of your backing. You went out on a limb. I mean it. What specifically do you want me to do?"

"Get your health back. There's a mountain of reading material heading your way. Then, tomorrow morning I want you at a 7:00 a.m. meeting. We have to make some crucial calls then."

They got up. Clay sneezed, grabbed for his handkerchief.

"I think a complete rest is in order for you once this is over."

"You mean Outward Bound?"

"You're not in any shape to go to Outward Bound. Like I said, go home. Take it easy, read all the material on Global."

They walked toward the door of P.J.'s.

"Shit, Dennis, I forgot. What's happening with you and Sandy? Did you talk to her? Did you ask her out?"

O'Brien headed north on Madison Avenue, turned back. "I did, sort of. The other night. I'll tell you about it, later." He gave Clay a wave, kept walking.

. . .

San Sebastian

Murphy stepped out on the deck surrounding the condo. The wood smelled fresh from the coat of stain that had been applied. He could see the ocean to the east, the mountains to the west. The lights from the town shown off to the south. He felt at home, pleased that he had convinced agency management that renting the condo was cheaper than a hotel. Sparrow had helped. The Minister had arranged the deal at minimum cost to the agency.

He'd brought along extra business and informal wear which he would leave in the apartment. He'd included several of his pistols in the baggage he'd checked at the airport. That way they were not seen by airport security. When he could do so, he planned on extending his business trips to San Sebastian into leisure time, having meetings on Friday, staying over on Saturday. It would give him some time to shoot, more time with Regina. As an investor in the condo complex, and with his increased fortunes, he would aim toward extended stays on the island.

He was eager to meet with Ramon to propose his plan for moving the account to Comnet. In his next conversation with Spiro Bates he would break the news that the San Sebastian account would be moving to his agency. Bates had struck gold to get both Global and the tourism business without effort. He would tell Bates that he would bring in the second account under his original financial deal. He didn't want to get greedy. Bates would be grateful to Murphy.

The Minister would see the wisdom of moving the account now that Murphy was off Global. It would be foolish for Ramon to take the risk of Murphy being dismissed from Burns & Cody. If that were to occur, Murphy would have a tough time getting a senior position at another agency. For the Minister to find a new conspirator at Burns & Cody would be difficult. The agency would assign someone to replace Murphy, someone the Minister didn't know. It would be touchy to suggest a kickback to a stranger. Plus, the Minister didn't know Sparrow, didn't know how the checks to him were handled. It would be much smarter for the Minister to stick with Murphy. He wished his father were alive to see all the deals that Murphy had cooking. Big time. Big money, not carnival wages.

It was going to be simple for Murphy to move the business to Comnet, where he now had a friend in Spiro Bates. Murphy checked his watch, he was due for his meeting with the Minister. He took the elevator down to the lobby, found a cab immediately.

The heat of the island was unusually enervating. O'Brien had joked that the record low for San Sebastian was 65°. Murphy paid the driver for the short ride, carried his suit coat slung over his shoulder, his tie loose, collar open. The coolness of the bar was a welcome refrigerator. As much as he disliked the public nature of the place, it had become a familiar and friendly meeting spot. He associated it with Regina and with the money that the Minister gave him.

For a change, the Minister was there ahead of him. The girl sat in the booth alone, watching the Minister entertaining his friends at the bar. Murphy could see there were a lot of empty glasses on the bar. When the Minister spotted Murphy he headed for the booth, smiled at Murphy as he approached. Murphy's eyes strayed only briefly from the girl's breasts as he greeted Ramon, sitting next to her. She wore a tight bathing suit top and a split skirt. His mind leapt ahead to later that evening.

"What's the matter, Murphy, all of your blood leave your brain? How about a cocktail?" He shouted to the waitress, circling his hand in the air, two fingers up. He put one arm around the girl's shoulders and squeezed. "*Salud*, my friend, it's been a while. Tell me what's happening on Madison Avenue."

"There have been better days. The airline crunch is still on, and I'm not sure where I stand at the agency. I'm off Global."

"I'm sorry to hear that, I hope it doesn't effect our little deal. By the way, slide your case over here and grab mine."

"It could. Big agencies don't pay people a lot of money to run a single fifteen million dollar account."

"I wouldn't worry about that. I always tell your creative director, what's his name, O'Brien, what a great job you do, how you're indispensable to us. I'm sure they'll give you another account or two."

"I doubt it, which leads me to an idea I have. It's something I've been thinking about for some time."

The Minister stopped smiling. "An idea. What idea?"

"What would you say to the thought of moving the account to a new agency? We could keep our deal running same as now."

"I think that's a dumb fucking idea. I like the way things are. Everything's smooth. You do great advertising for us and everybody makes *mucho dinero*. Why change that?"

"I think you should consider it. Besides, we're partners, aren't we? I also think that we should kick up the payments. More for you and more for me."

The Minister knocked over his glass, grabbed the girl's arm, jolting her upward. "Regina, why don't you take a nice walk?" He leaned toward Murphy. "Are you fucking crazy? Where are you getting these ideas? You're getting greedy, aren't you Murphy? What's the matter, is your gambling out of control? I'm happy with the current deal. If the billings go up again, maybe we can talk about an increase. That's my call. By the way, what's this partnership bullshit? Since when do you have a say? This is my game and I can take it anywhere I want. You're lucky to be in the game at all." The group at the bar stared at the booth.

Murphy sat up. "What makes you think you can order me around? I know a lot, you know."

The Minister moved too fast for Murphy. He grabbed his tie and yanked it toward him. Murphy's head hit the table hard. The Minister took hold of Murphy's hair, pulled his head up. Red liquid, darker than his hair, trickled from his forehead. "There are no partners. You're just a tool for me. One call to the agency and you're history." He squeezed Murphy's necktie, pulled his head within inches of his own. Murphy's eyes watered from his whiskey breath. "Don't ever threaten me. Some day I'll play the tapes I have of you, let you hear what a noisy lover you are. 'Oh, *Señor* Murphy, don't stop now.' Or, send the tapes home so your wife and kids can hear how hard Daddy works when he's on the road." He squeezed tighter. "Don't fuck with me. I have ways of dealing with troublemakers, believe me." He let go of Murphy, got up from the table and walked to the bar. "Drinks for everyone, *mi amigos*." The girl passed him on her way back to the booth.

Murphy looked over at the Minister laughing with the group at the bar. Then, the bar began its nightly transformation. The lights started flashing, mirrors moving, music pounding. Before the girl could sit down Murphy grabbed the briefcase, headed for the door. The girl glanced at the Minister, followed Murphy out.

• • •

DAY 9

The Plaza Hotel

The Oak Room bar at the Plaza Hotel was practically empty, just two middle-aged men at a table in the back. It looked to O'Brien like they were holding hands. He decided to sit at the bar. He hoped that she would meet him. It was clear from their brief telephone conversation that she had been very upset by the scene in his office. What had happened had been as big a surprise to him as it was to Sandy. Did she think that it was part of his routine, hitting on unsuspecting women in his office?

He wasn't sure what he was going to tell her, except he knew he was in love and he wanted her to know that. He had no way of predicting what her reaction might be. As he reflected on what had happened in the office, as brief as it was, it was clear to him that there had been a strong response by her to his advances. It seemed that she had been torn between letting go and resisting him. Could it be that she was interested in him? It had all happened so fast that there had been no time for either of them to think about what was going on.

The two men left together. They were holding hands and didn't seem to care who saw them. He ordered another beer. It was almost 7:00 p.m., she must have decided not to come, decided not to ever meet him. It was over before it began. Just as this idea began to sink in, Sandy arrived. He jumped off the chair to greet her. She was beautiful. He wanted to take her in his arms and kiss her and tell her he loved her.

"You look lonely, all by yourself in this big room."

"I didn't think you would come." Nervous, he helped her onto one of the huge bar stools.

"The copy meeting went on and on, Kreeger confused about what the advertising was supposed to do. I feel sorry for him, he's completely out of place. He doesn't know anything about the subject of advertising, he just has a bunch of questions. I'd swear he isn't even listening to our answers. Incidentally, they wanted to know where you were. This was my first copy meeting at Global without you there to prop me up."

"I'm sure it went great. Like I said, it's a chance for them to get to know you better, to have confidence in you before the big blowout. Did they buy anything?"

"They bought everything in the bag. Ted Crowther is as good as Kreeger is bad. But, you must have had something big to do to keep you from a Global meeting."

"I'll tell you about it in a minute, but first I want to talk about the other night."

"I don't know what happened the other night."

"Do you think I planned it, do you think I go around seducing people in my office?"

"No, I don't. I believe you when you tell me it just happened. But, as for some of the things that you said on the phone, how you feel about me, I think that was also in the heat of the moment. We don't know each other."

He moved around on the bar stool uneasily, looked at her. "That's not really true, we do know each other, we've worked together more or less for years. I'm just beginning to realize how strongly I feel about you ... that I'm in love with you, Sandy." He held his hand up to prevent her from interrupting. "I'm sure of it, there's not even a shred of doubt in my mind. The event in my office happened, but I was getting around to telling you my feelings anyway, it just speeded things up."

"I'm flabbergasted ... " She paused, looked around the empty room. "Dennis, let's be clear about this. You're a married man. I was married once, happily married. I guess I'd like to be married again. One thing I'm sure of, I'm not interested in having an affair with a married man. I know all kinds of things go on these days, but I'm not going to get involved. Plus, you're my boss, which makes it ten times worse. Everything I was taught, everything I believe in, prevents me from going out with you. Not that I don't find you attractive, I guess you could tell that from how I reacted, but it's something that I can't do. It won't work. Plus, we've got just ten days left to save Global. That should be the only thing on our minds."

"I didn't say anything about an affair, did I? I wanted to meet you today for two reasons. I wanted you to know that I love you and I wanted you to know that I'm already midway into divorce proceedings. That's where I just came from, my lawyer's office."

"I'm sorry to hear that."

"My marriage has been finished for years, but I never got around to doing anything about it. I've been lonely for a long time, something's been missing. Some time, if you'll hear me out, I'll explain the whole situation to you, what happened and why, at least to the degree I understand it." He reached over and took her hand. "I really am crazy about you."

"Dennis, damn it, don't tell me you're getting a divorce because of me."

"I'm getting a divorce because it's time for my wife and I to do it. It's independent of my feelings toward you."

"Dennis, all of this is happening a little too fast for me. I have to repeat, you're my boss. We have a lot of work to do in the next week, the whole damn agency's on the line. I think we should postpone these kinds of conversations."

"You're right, but you must understand that it was important that I tell you how I feel. I couldn't keep it to myself any longer." He took both of her hands in his. "Promise me you'll consider this once we've given the presentation. I want you to understand how I feel."

She turned toward him. "Dennis, look, you've got to promise me you won't talk about this at all, until the presentation is over."

"Great! After the presentation, then." He stood up. "Now, where are you heading? I'll get you a taxi."

In front of the Plaza there was the usual line of cabs. He helped her into one, reached in through the open window to take her hand, letting go only as the cab pulled off. She looked back at him, half smiling, shaking her head.

. . .

San Sebastian

Murphy ran his finger across his forehead, felt the indentation from the cut. It was sore, but didn't appear to be large. He couldn't see his watch in the dark of the bedroom, but it must be morning. He reached over and turned on the light. It was 7:00 a.m. The girl stirred next to him. "How would you like to come to New York for a few days?"

She squinted at him, half asleep, gradually sat up, the sheet sliding away. "New York? What are you talking about?"

"Come to New York. I'll pay for the trip. You want to become a model. I can tell you that you're prettier than most of them, and I can help. I can give you the connections you need. Believe me. You'd have a great time. You're young. You don't want to spend the rest of your life on this island working for him. A pretty girl has to take advantage of her looks when she's young. You're damn smart. You know that's true. Besides, he's bad, an evil man, a wild man. I couldn't believe last night. He was crazed."

"He was drunk. Normally, he's not that much of a drinker, but he had been with his friends all afternoon." She stood up, went to the window, peeked out. "But, the way you're talking about me coming to New York would never work. The Minister would never let me go. I know too much, so do you for that matter. He's a powerful man and what power he doesn't have his friends in the government do. He gets people involved in his schemes, then he takes advantage of them. It was his idea to tape us in bed, so that he could use it against you if he had to. Getting you into the condo deal was another way. It's corrupt and now you're part of it.

"There are a lot of people on the island under his control. They start out like me, poor with no hope. You get to have some fun, you learn a lot, go to places you'd never dreamed of, make some money, real money. Next thing you know you're in deep, you'd like to get out, but you can't, he won't let you. I know him too well. He's threatened to kill me. You've seen the gun he carries, well, he's used it more than once. He acts like your best friend, but he's your enemy because he has control of the most important thing of all, your freedom. He will hold the tapes over your head as a threat, forever. He will want you to do things you never imagined. You'll regret having ever met him."

She got out of bed, put on a robe. "Now that you had this fight in public he will do whatever it takes to keep you under his control. Your life will become a nightmare of fear. I know it, because I live it. And I know plenty of others in the same situation. I laugh when I see the beautiful commercials you make, showing the island as a paradise with all the friendly natives, when I know that the people that control the island, like the Minister, are devils on earth. I could tell you stories that would make you shiver in fear.

"After last night he will want to change your deal, just to demonstrate his control over you. He will squeeze you for the pure pleasure of it, and he will tell his friends so that they can all have a good laugh at your expense. And if you don't go along he will get violent like he started to get last night. He has the temper of a maniac. I've seen it. He will try to change your arrangement, maybe take you up on your idea to move the account, but he'll move it and cut you out. Then, he'll think of some way to use you because he has the tapes. Go to New York? I'll never leave this island as long as he's alive. You can count on it. In fact, after tonight, he will forbid me from ever seeing you again, because it will no longer be necessary for his purposes. I can see it coming."

Murphy got out of bed, went to her, held her against him. "If I could figure a way to get rid of him, would you come to New York?"

She fell back on the bed. "Get rid of him, what are you saying? This is crazy talk, who do you think you are? You've seen too many movies. But, this is real. You're way over your head here. You're no match for him. He's too tough."

"Wait a minute. Let's talk about this. You're saying he has control of your life and you don't like it, that you're trapped. You're saying he has me, too, and I believe you. I don't want to live like that. Look, I'm about to make a lot of money, more than you can conceive. The set-up with the Minister is chicken feed in comparison. We're talking millions. I'm changing agencies, with a big five year payoff. I'm about to make a bundle in a stock deal. I don't need the Minister anymore. It would have been nice to move our arrangement to another agency, keep going like nothing happened. But, it's not in the cards." He stood up, walked over to the window. "Well, it's not in the cards for him to hold those tapes over my head. What a cheap trick, those tapes."

"He made me do it, I told you. But, now, I'm sure you know, I've gotten to like you. I don't have to pretend anymore." She walked over next to him, kissed him on the ear.

"I'm not blaming you for the tapes. You're young and he took advantage of you. What I'm saying is I'm willing to pay big money to get rid of this man, do the whole damn island a service. Neither one of us would ever have to worry about him and his control."

"You're crazy to even think about it. It's out of the question and it would cost too much, anyway."

"The money part is not a problem, I can pay whatever it takes. Say, fifty large, fifty grand. There must be ways to do these things on the island. You know a lot of people here. He must have enemies, someone who'd be willing to do it for us, someone you can trust."

"For fifty grand you don't have to find an enemy. But, I'm still afraid. Forget the whole idea, if you're smart."

He took her in his arms. "How can I forget about it after what's happened, after what you've told me? I want you to think about this, work on it. Call me when I get back to New York. Then, I'll find you a great apartment, a place to live in New York. You can put all this business behind you." He pulled her against him. "We'll have fun like you won't believe. New York's the greatest city in the world if you have the money to enjoy it. The people will go wild over you. And only you and I will know what happened."

. . .

Westfield, New Jersey

Clay Walker sat in the den at his mother-in-law's. His wife had talked him into the trip. He had agreed to have dinner in Westfield as long as they would return home that evening.

Clay had brought a fifth of Cutty Sark for the occasion and had it with him in the den, but he was still too sick to drink. He hadn't felt well since his night in Grand Central.

He spread the New York Times across his lap. The front page, to Clay, was the best available diary on the state of the world. He had developed a system for categorizing each of the front page stories as a barometer of conditions. He had chosen six categories for which he awarded a plus or a minus for civilization depending on the drift of the stories that appeared. Each day, as an escape, Clay tried to find the time to go through this exercise. He had selected War and Peace, Economics, Freedom, Health, Crime, and Arts and Sciences as his six indicators. On any given day there was front page news related to several of the categories, rarely was there news about all six.

This day there was only one story related to War and Peace, some fighting between ethnic groups in Albania. A day did not go by without fighting of some kind, somewhere. He scored one minus.

There were two crime stories, one local and one about a bribe scandal in Washington. The first announced the arrest of another huge drug cartel. Millions of dollars in cocaine had been confiscated. There was obviously no end to the supplies of drugs and of people willing to risk their lives for the enormous potential gains. The government would never be able to cut off the supplies and the country was too hypocritical to legalize drugs.

Clay's wife and mother-in-law entered the nearby living room, their conversation momentarily interrupting Clay's game. "Wasn't that good of Clay to take such good care of Felix after the funeral?" he heard his mother-in-law say.

"He was very fond of Father." This from his wife.

Clay returned to his studies. He put a minus in the crime column. There was a major story about the progress toward defining the tiniest elements of matter. Colliders in Europe and the U.S. had enough computer-generated pictures of the fallout of extraordinary high speed collisions of particles to conclude that the most fundamental elements of nature could be understood. There was a smaller adjoining article about how the Hubbel telescope was helping science look back fourteen billion years, to the beginning of time. A big plus day for Arts and Science. He coughed, blew his nose. He was reaching the bottom of the big Kleenex box he had bought the day before.

"Where do you think we should put Felix? Maybe we should spread his ashes over the campus of the university."

There was nothing else relevant on the front page. He totaled up the score sheet. Like most days, a slight minus.

He turned his mind to more practical matters, what was happening at the agency and how it might affect him. If the agency somehow managed to keep the Global account, as O'Brien thought it would, it would be hard to deny O'Brien the presidency. If that happened the implications for Clay were clear and positive. Adding Global to his long list of clients and reporting directly to the new president would place him in the highest echelons of the agency. Clearly, keeping the Global account represented the biggest opportunity of his career. He was going to throw himself into the situation to try to do anything he could in the next week to influence events.

Suddenly, he felt much sicker, the virus or whatever it was, began to effect his stomach. He stood up, headed for the living room.

"What if we put the urn on the mantle? Don't you think that would be the best place for now? Here's Clay. Clay, what do you think? We're ... "

Clay let out a piercing shriek as he collapsed straight down. He writhed on the floor, his face contorted in a convulsion, his body shaking toward a crescendo, then no movement at all.

Clay's wife knelt by him, screaming, "Call 911, call 911, Mother, hurry, he's dying!"

• • •

DAY 8

O'Grady's Bar, Eighth Avenue

Murphy stood in the doorway, looked up and down the street before he turned into the bar, a dingy, dark spot on Eighth Avenue. He had picked as obscure a meeting place as possible. It would be hard to explain to someone from the agency what he was doing with Kreeger now that he was off the account. The chairman had been explicit about the speed of change from him to Clay Walker, although for some reason Walker had not returned his phone calls. The bar would be empty at this time of day, eliminating any chance of being overheard. He paid the bartender for a beer and took it to a small wooden table in the back of the unoccupied room, took out his cigarettes and his meeting notes.

He savored the taste of the cool liquid, lit a cigarette. He was pleased with the way things were progressing. Regina had called from the island and amazed him with all the details of a plan to eliminate the Minister. For such a young girl she had the savvy and the contacts to get things done. It was agreed that Murphy would return to San Sebastian in two days to deliver the money and to obtain proof that the Minister had been killed. It would mean the end of the payoffs on the account, but he had a new, bigger source of money heading his way from Comnet. The affair with the Minister had always made him uneasy. And, being in collusion with Steve Sparrow meant another person knew about the deal. But, it had been the only way to get agency checks to the Minister. The Minister's death would be a visible explanation to Sparrow that their arrangement was over. Besides, Murphy would be at Comnet by then.

At Comnet and rich. Richer than he had ever imagined. Plus, there were the stock options on Global that would pay off at any minute. He had more action going than ever in his life. So much action that he hadn't even bothered on making any basketball bets in the last few days. When you were about to make millions, what were a few thousand dollars on a basketball game? That was small potatoes compared to his other action.

His father had never come close to a big payoff, had died penniless. Murphy would make sure that his own kids would have a better life, would never know about their grandfather, would never know how their own father had hit it big.

He made out the large silhouette of Kreeger as he entered the bar, and followed the pointing finger of the bartender toward the back of the room.

"Hi, Jack, I'm glad you could meet me. It's important, as you'll see."

"It's kind of a strange place to meet. I didn't know if I'd hear from you. We got the letter saying you were off the business and that someone named Clay Walker was coming on. I guess he's sick or something. He was supposed to come over to the airline today, but the meeting was canceled. What's he like?"

"He's good. No airline experience though."

"I guess we'll just have to see." Kreeger looked uneasy.

"Would you like a drink, Jack?" Murphy waved at the bartender to come over.

"Sure, a Coke's fine, but tell me why you wanted to meet in such a weird place."

Murphy called the bartender over, ordered a Coke and another beer. As soon as they were alone, he looked over at Kreeger. "Jack, what I have to say to you is very important. It could have a dramatic effect on the way you live."

"I don't get it."

"Let me explain. First, it's pretty certain that the agency is going to be fired by Bill Swenson."

"I don't know that for sure, Malachy. He's never said that directly to me."

"C'mon, Jack, it's all over the airline that Swenson's trying to take over. He's made himself visible everywhere. The agency's just another part. And the way I figure it he's got the votes: your's, Baxter's, Fran Irwin's, to get the job done."

"I don't know that either."

"Let's say that you and the other two guys like their jobs. It wouldn't be smart to go against your boss."

Kreeger looked at Murphy, said nothing.

"O.K., the next thing I hear, there's going to be a second agency in the picture, that Comnet's been called to pitch the account."

Kreeger squirmed in his seat, avoided looking at Murphy. "How ... why do you say that?"

"Look, Jack, I'm not asking you to tell me something that you're supposed to keep secret. But, this kind of big news is hard to keep under wraps. Let's just say that I know about Comnet and drop it at that."

Kreeger looked at him, quiet.

"Let's assume for a minute, whether you agree or not, that next week a vote's going to be taken and Comnet's going to be Global's new agency. Just assume it for the purpose of discussion."

"Yeh."

"My question to you is how protected is Jack Kreeger going to be in the new situation? Somebody could make the argument that Swenson only put you in the advertising job so he could control what was happening, so that he could arrange the agency change with the advertising director's help. It couldn't have been that you were put in the job because of your advertising experience, since you don't have any. I'm not being critical, Jack. I'm just saying a guy like Swenson, a guy who loves power, wanted to make sure he could get the votes he needed to change agencies and it was easier having someone who didn't know anything about advertising, didn't have a strong point of view on agency matters, someone like you as ad director, to make it easier to make the change." He took a long drink from the beer bottle.

"Well, maybe that's true, but what of it?"

"I'm just saying, at Global these days, where you have a respected older chairman and a younger hard-charging guy who wants to take over, that the younger guy, Swenson, has to smooth the way as much as possible to swing things to his side. He just can't jump in and take over, the board wouldn't let him. It's got to happen in a fair, democratic looking way. So, he gets changes by moving people around the airline into places where they can help him. You're not the only one who moved into a strange job based on past experience."

"I guess that's true, but I don't see where this leads."

"It could lead to a situation, once the agency change is a done deal, where Swenson decides to put a professional ad man in your job. Swenson's a good business man. Wouldn't he want the most capable person in every key position?"

"Maybe."

"I'm suggesting that your job may not be secure, that you could be in jeopardy."

"I'm not sure that I agree, but what if I am?"

"Jack, look at me." Murphy leaned forward, lowered his voice. "While you're still the ad director you can influence some things, you have the power to help others and to help yourself."

"I don't get it."

"Let me be specific. When Comnet gets selected they're going to need someone to run the Global account."

"Sure, of course ... I mean, if that were to happen."

"Well, I want to be that person. I want to go over to Comnet and keep running the Global business. I've got the experience, I know all the Global people, and in all modesty, I know that the people at Global think highly of me. Every evaluation the agency has gotten has put me as one of the two or three agency people important to the account."

"I guess that's so."

"It is. So isn't it smart for the airline to bring over their own agency guy to the new agency? It will make for a smooth transition. No balls will be dropped. It makes complete business sense. It's the kind of decision that a guy like Swenson would appreciate."

"Maybe you're right."

"I am. That's why I want you to make that recommendation to Swenson. At the appropriate time of course. I've even written a draft of a letter for you to send to Swenson, providing the arguments for moving me to Comnet." He handed the letter to Kreeger. "Now, here's the most important part. If you do this, and it happens, I'm willing to reward you for your help."

"Reward?"

"That's right. For your help I'd be willing to pay you fifty thousand dollars, cash."

Kreeger's head jerked back against the back of the bench.

"You're right, Jack, it's a lot of money. But, think of this as a business arrangement. You get some insurance money to protect you against what might happen if you were given a smaller job or even fired. And I get to keep the job I've had for the last five years, only at a different agency. And, this is important. It's good for Global, they avoid any screw-ups when they change agencies. Fifty large. Cash, Jack. You just put it in your pocket and no one's any wiser. Just a little deal between two business men, you and me."

"I'm confused. I have to think ... "

"Sure you do, Jack. I want you to. And I'm sure you'll conclude that making a recommendation that's in the best interests of the airline makes sense. And in this job market, with airlines going belly up right and left, a man's got to protect himself. I'm not saying Swenson's a bad man, but I don't imagine he gives a rat's ass about the future of Jack Kreeger. He hardly knows you. You're just one of the thousands of people at the airline. And one other thing. Your assistant, Mary Carey is smart, experienced and one gorgeous lady. Don't you think Swenson hasn't noticed her? So give it a good think, and I'm sure you'll decide to support me. There's no downside and the fifty grand cash is tax free. A man's got to work a lot of years to put away that kind of cash."

They walked together toward the front door of the bar. Out in the entry way, in the light, Kreeger's ears were more prominent than usual. "Say, Jack, since we're going to be business partners can I make a personal suggestion?"

"Sure, what is it?"

"We all know you're always trying to make your ears stay back, that you're sensitive about them. Why don't you take some of the cash you're getting and spend it on some cosmetic surgery. I'm sure they can straighten those ears out for you."

Kreeger brightened. "Do you really think so? Do you know the name of a doctor who could do that?"

"Let me work on it. I'll call you." He shook his hand, prepared for Kreeger's aggressive grip. "You leave first, Jack. There's no point in our being seen together. I'll call you soon."

Murphy watched Kreeger's cab disappear. The part about the ears had been the icing on the cake. Kreeger couldn't refuse the deal. Within a week Murphy would be at Comnet, rich, with a beautiful, young mistress at his side.

• • •

DAY 7

Burns & Cody

O'Brien handed his secretary some mail, stepped back into his office. "You can't have a campaign without a campaign theme. How can you have a musical commercial if there's no slogan? How do you end the commercial, any commercial? How do you sell a new campaign to a client if you have no theme?" O'Brien slammed his right hand against the top of his desk.

"The truth is you don't." Sandy's eyes followed him as he paced around the room. She had never seen him so intense. He'd never been tested like this. How many times had he been the leader the agency relied on in a crisis? How many times had he come to the help of people personally? In her own case, after her husband died, he'd been caring, empathetic, ready to give her as much time as she needed to get back to work. She looked at the photos on the wall, pictures of him laughing with his son. She would like to bring that laughter back to his face, to make him ...

O'Brien hit both hands on top of his desk. "In the history of the advertising business there's never been a campaign without a slogan. You're supposed to come up with the theme line before you develop any of the parts of the campaign. The theme is the focal point. And what do we have?"

"Mostly bits and pieces, Dennis, but a lot of them. We have several excellent ideas for commercials, some outstanding music, a bunch of terrific magazine and newspaper ads, all on the bigness is goodness strategy, but no ... "

"No theme line."

O'Brien's secretary came into the office. She gave Sandy a quick glance, turned to O'Brien. "Clay Walker's on the phone."

"Sandy, will you give me a couple of minutes? I need to talk to Clay." He waited until the two had departed, sat down on his hammock, phone in hand. "Clay, what's going on, you're in the hospital? Cathy called me and told me what happened."

"If you talked to Cathy you know. They tell me I had a convulsion, an alcohol withdrawal fit. I was so sick, you saw me on Monday, I couldn't drink. We came here to New Jersey, to my mother-in-law's for dinner and I felt worse. The thought of booze, or food for that matter, was out. I didn't know how dependent my system had grown to alcohol. When it didn't have any for a couple of days I had a violent reaction, a fit. They've explained it to me here at the hospital. What happened is not that unusual for people who drink a lot. If someone in my situation had gone to rehab, they would have weaned me off alcohol, detoxed me, so that there wouldn't have been a violent reaction."

"It must have scared the hell out of you."

"I don't remember any of it. Cathy's gone to great lengths to describe it to me though."

"How serious was the attack?"

"Do you mean are there any lasting effects? It doesn't look that way. In a lot of cases there are, effects on the brain, you know. I was lucky. People have been known to die from these fits, or have severe side effects. I'm still learning about it."

"You're telling me you had a body that was used to having a lot of alcohol in it, and when it didn't, it reacted."

"That's their conclusion."

"Is there anything you need? What's supposed to happen next?"

"I'm supposed to stay in detox another day. Then, I'm supposed to enter the dependency program that adjoins the hospital."

"What's that all about?"

"Just what you might think, it's a thirty day alcohol abuse program, tied into AA."

"It sounds like that's what you should do, my friend."

"The first thing is to get out of detox, out of the hospital itself. Next, there's a lot of pressure from the people here, and my family, to go straight to rehab. My brother flew in from Denver to be part of this. The idea is to accept that I have a problem and take steps to deal with it."

"You've always kidded about rehab."

"Yeah, like a lot of jokes, there was some truth to it. To be honest, I knew I drank a lot, but I never saw myself as addicted to the stuff. But, out here they ask you a lot of questions, like when was the last day before I got sick when I hadn't had a drink."

"And?"

"I couldn't remember, as hard as I tried. I guess I've been hooked for a long time."

"Look, you should do what they say. It sounds to me like this could turn into a good thing."

"Dennis, the optimist. But, maybe you're right. Tell me what's going on with the airline. Weren't you and I supposed to go to Global today?"

"True."

"What did you tell them?"

"I said we had to postpone the meeting until you felt better, that you had a virus."

"Out here they call it the Irish virus. What did Global say?"

"Nothing, what could they say?"

"Hey, Dennis, this puts the agency in a strange position. You write a letter introducing the new guy and it turns out he's in rehab. A hell of way to save the account."

"You take care of yourself, we'll take care of the airline."

"It looks to me like you have less than a week left and you have no account guy. Plus, I was in charge of one of the shoots."

"We'll send someone else. I want you to follow instructions like a good Marine. Take it easy, O.K.?"

"Right, I'll call you later."

O'Brien put the phone down at the bottom of the hammock, walked from his office. "Evelyn, where did Sandy go?"

"Sandy? I haven't any idea. I guess she got tired of waiting."

He crossed in front of his secretary's desk, walked down the hall to Sandy's office. "Sorry, where were we?"

"We were bemoaning the fact that we have no theme line. I was going to say, out of the dozens of lines that have been suggested, there are several that are workable, not great, but usable if we have to."

"Well, we'd better review them again. I'd say by midnight tomorrow we have to make a call. We've got to mix the music and start integrating all the parts. We can't do that without a theme. Meanwhile, let's do one last memo to the entire creative department asking for ideas."

"Fine, but you know the answer is unlikely to come from anyone who's not involved in the business. It never does."

"You're right. Skip it. It was a desperate thought from a desperate man. Now, another thing. Each of us was going to handle one of the TV shoots and Clay was going to do the third. It looks like he's too sick to go, so think of somebody else to cover it."

"Fine, what else?"

"Tomorrow night we look at all the work, theme lines, commercials, print ads, outdoor, radio, the works. We decide on which ideas make it. From then on it's a production job. I assume everyone knows they have to work all weekend."

"We're going to have to give everyone an extra holiday when this is over."

O'Brien got up to leave. "I'm planning on a massive all night party next week, when Global decides to stay."

Sandy ran her fingers through her hair. "That would be quite a party, wouldn't it?"

. . .

San Sebastian

The girl stood in front of the full length mirror, holding the phone. She moved from side to side, admiring her reflection. "Hello, Ramon, wait till you hear this, you won't believe it." She listened, swaying back and forth, fascinated with the movement of her breasts. "He bought the whole story. He's coming here, and he's bringing the money, cash. He didn't blanch at the hundred G's. Can you believe it? What are you planning for him? Are you going to take care of him? I could make the arrangements. Why don't you let me handle it? When do you want me to meet you?"

She leaned back on the bed, arranged the pillows behind her head, reviewed her plan once more. It was one the Minister would be pleased with. There were many things she had learned from him. Looking back, it had been an intense three year education. He had picked her up in a bar, fallen for her, promised her a new life. He'd delivered on his promise, and more. Her drab life, with few prospects except prostitution, had suddenly become glamourous.

From the start she had no delusions about what she had done. Her mother had told her she was a whore, only a high priced one. Well, if a woman had to take advantage of her chief asset, why not use it to link up with a powerful politician. A rich one and a handsome one to boot. But, Ramon had quickly grown tired of their lovemaking, had moved on to other island girls. There were plenty of them available to a man of his importance. But, instead of abandoning her like the others before, he had kept her on, told her he saw a talent in her that she, herself, was barely aware of, her brains. Like most islanders, school had been a sometime and short-lived part of her youth. Early on, she had looked for a way to maximize her looks. She'd never thought much about the level of her intelligence. Until Ramon had enlightened her.

One of the things she had learned from him was how to plan and think things through. His life was a collection of schemes, each of which relied to some degree on deception. He had told her that to succeed you had to carefully plot out all the steps, cover all the bases, make sure if you were duping someone that they would never catch on, and if they did, that they would pay the price for their stupidity.

She had become apprentice to a master of corruption, and then a full accomplice in all his activities, even a creative resource for him. In the process he'd taken ownership of her. What she'd told Murphy was true, that the Minister controlled her, told her what to do, where to go, that the thought of her escaping his bondage was absurd.

What Murphy had suggested, the elimination of the Minister was an idea she had entertained herself. The Minister, as important as he was on the island, as rich as he had become, had weaknesses that she was sure would undo him. And, it would serve her purposes, her desire to be free of him, if his weaknesses led to his downfall.

One weakness was his drinking. The drunker he got, the more dangerous he became — not just to others, but to himself. His extreme behavior had the affect of weakening his thinking processes, leading to mistakes of judgment, errors of communication. The incident with Murphy was one of several examples, because it hadn't been necessary to antagonize Murphy, to harm his physically, to make him an enemy. A smarter, soberer person could have handled Murphy without the violence, without the hate. Murphy wasn't as smart as he thought he was.

The Minister had unknowingly taught her the danger of arrogance, as well. What could happen when you thought you were invulnerable. He had shown her the risk of trusting someone too much, letting your guard down, thinking that you were beyond the boundaries that most people live by. That weakness and that lesson was one she knew he would live to regret. The student was now in the position to teach the professor a lesson in mortality.

She got up, turned on the CD, a samba. She stood in front of the mirror and moved to the beat of the music, pleased with her appearance, more pleased with the beauty of her plan. The Minister would be proud of her, proud of his pupil, except he wouldn't be able to savor his success.

• • •

DAY 6

Westfield General Hospital

She was a big-busted nurse, "Charlene" on her name tag. "Just relax, Mr. Walker, I'm going to remove your IV. You won't be needing it anymore. You'll probably be a little wobbly. How do you feel?"

"I'll feel great when you get that out. It's like being tied down." He wiggled his freed arm around, examined the mark from the needle.

"The rehab doctor will be here soon, a Dr. Natchez. Here are your clothes, you can put them on whenever you like. The doctor will be taking you over to our rehab unit next door."

He watched her leave, picked up the phone. "Information, do you have the number of a taxi company in Westfield? Any taxi company ... Thanks." He reached for the clothes the nurse had put on the bed, dialed with his free hand. "Hello, would you please send a cab right away to the main entrance of Westfield General Hospital. Right, my name is Walker and I'll be going to the city, New York ... yes, the city, midtown. Thanks. I'm ready right now."

He wasn't prepared for the dizziness when he stood up. He staggered to the wall, propped himself against it, his head resting on his crossed arms. What the hell had they put in that IV and the pills they'd been loading him up with? He pushed hard on the wall with his hands, straightened up. He stood in place, shook his head, looking for equilibrium. He considered resting a moment on the bed, but remembered the doctor was due, then the cab. He moved out the door, shuffled down the hallway, followed the signs for the elevator, avoided the eyes of the passers-by. A nursing station stood in his path. He edged his way around it, the nurses backs toward him.

"Which way to Walker's room?"

Clay watched the doctor through a large plant between him and the nurses' station. He could read "Dr. Natchez" on his ID. The doctor looked over, peered over his glasses, then turned to complete his mission to Clay's room.

The elevator took forever. He eased his way to the back, rested against the wall. Was it his imagination or were elevators in hospitals geared to be slow?

Outside, the sun stung his eyes. Could just two days of incapacitation do this to his body? He leaned against a large oak, away from the busy entrance. He had a clear line of sight of the main road into the hospital. Minutes later, the cab, its bright yellow reflected in the glare, wound its way toward him. He could make out "Westfield" on the roof fixture. With one hand on the tree, he summoned the car with the other. The driver stopped, got out of the car. "Are you Mr. Walker?"

Clay let go of the tree, spun, fell against the car.

"Are you all right, Buddy?" He opened the door, eased Clay down.

"I'm great, my friend, just get me to New York City the fastest way you know."

. . .

East 83rd Street

Kat nestled against her, purring. She rubbed the cat's neck with one hand, wrote with the other. This was the fourth or fifth rewrite of her opening remarks. The chairman would begin the presentation with a brief introduction of the agency attendees and a statement of commitment. Then, O'Brien was going to show a tape of the best commercials the agency had done for Global, a ten minute summation of ten years' work. The original plan had been to have Clay Walker follow O'Brien. Clay would deliver an explanation of the strategic foundation for the campaign that the agency would be showing. With Clay sick, O'Brien was planning on handling that part himself, although he said he would feel uncomfortable doing it. He had counted on Clay and his proven ability to make the subject of strategy into an exciting and dramatic element.

Following the strategic section, the main part of the presentation, the introduction of all the new creative material, had been given to Sandy. She hoped to put her opening remarks to memory, with a 3 by 5 card to be used only if absolutely necessary.

She was having trouble achieving the right blend of enthusiasm, sincerity and confidence. She had thought of asking Dennis to write the opening for her, but knew it would be a sign of weakness. If she hoped to become creative director she had to demonstrate her independence. Besides, the opening had to reflect her own thoughts, her own emotions, if it was going to have impact.

A television glowed in the corner of the room, the sound turned down. Out of the corner of her eye she caught the title, *Late Nite Theatre.* It was an old black and white movie, one she had seen many times over the years, a film starring Bing Crosby as a priest. She tried to remember if Bing had won an Academy

Award for it. She thought he had. Often she watched television with the sound down. She liked to observe the visual flow of the different programs and commercials, in order to study the transitions and assorted styles of the directors. It was easier to follow the visuals without any distracting sound. In contrast, but for similar reasons, she had observed O'Brien, eyes closed, listening to commercials in order to trace the flow of words unimpeded by the pictures.

Her mind drifted back to her brief experience with O'Brien in his office, to their conversation at the Plaza. She felt an attraction toward him, she knew that, but was confused as to what she should do. She remembered in his office how nice his lips had felt against hers, how he had awakened forgotten feelings in her. At the Plaza they had made a deal that they would not talk about it until the presentation was over. But, that was only six days away, six short days with so much to do.

She was drowsy, beyond being tired. The last three-and-a-half weeks had taken its toll. She tried to recall the various ideas that were options for the presentation, the desperate need for a theme line. She was half asleep. The TV flickered, signaling a break in the movie. Suddenly the idea was there. It struck her immediately as a good one, the right one at the right time. There was a rush of exhilaration. She freed herself from Kat, reached for the phone. "Dennis, you're still at the office? Good, I think I've got it. I'm coming right over."

. . .

San Sebastian

It was a picturesque penthouse condominium. From the broad living room area of the three bedroom suite the view encompassed a large semi-circular beach and the sea beyond. There were twenty identical apartments in the San Sebastian complex, which was at the furthest point of the island from the airport. Maynard Baxter and Fran Irwin were spending their second night on the island prior to flying back to New York. Fran had spent the two days on the island working out the details of the packages that Global would be offering from the complex. Both parties were satisfied with the agreement. With the additional customers generated by the airline, the condo owners felt confident that they would be able to achieve occupancy rates in the ninety percent range the following winter. Fran was convinced that the package prices for the condos would make them attractive to Global's flyers. She could see strong possibilities for summer packages as well.

Baxter had not been seen much during the daytime hours of the trip. Fran knew he had gone off with one of the girls that had magically appeared shortly after their arrival. The evening before, she had seen Baxter take the principal owner of the apartments out on the porch facing the beach. No doubt, Baxter had at that time received his cash kickback. Fran hadn't seen any money change hands, but the fact that Baxter had told Fran to go ahead and finalize the deal meant that Baxter was happy with the arrangement.

It was 7:30 p.m. and they were to be joined for dinner at 8:00 by several owners. Baxter and Fran were sitting in the living room having a drink. Baxter was smoking some hash, which one of the girls had gotten for him. He was smoking the black substance through a long, thin glass tube, inhaling the smoke and holding it in his lungs, in between sips from his rum and Coke.

"You know, Fran, the agency presentation is next week and we're expecting you to vote against the agency."

"What do you mean by 'we'?"

"Well, let's say that 'we' represents the group that will be running the airline starting soon, with Bill Swenson as chairman."

"You think so?" He was in a condescending mood, bolstered by the drugs.

"Fran, I don't think so, I know so."

"So, what if I vote to keep the agency? I've told you, in my opinion they've done a great job."

"Fran, you can vote for whoever you want, it's a free country. You'll really be free if you do." Baxter looked at her and laughed.

"What's that supposed to mean, another threat?"

"That's not a threat, that's a promise. If you don't vote with us, it's the same as voting against us, which means you don't want to be part of us. Pretty simple."

"I don't think that's the right way to do business. It's not fair."

"I'm sick of your moralizing, your goody, goody act. Giving me the evil eye all the time. You work for me and you do what I say, or else. That should be clear. Here, make me another Cuba libre." He pushed the glass toward her, took a drag from the tube.

Fran took the glass and turned away. She felt on the verge of some form of violent retaliation. She didn't know what to do. She headed toward the bar just as three owners appeared in the kitchen doorway. They had let themselves in through the back of the apartment.

"Hey, look who's here," yelled Baxter. "Right on time. Fran and I were just concluding some high level business discussions, right Fran?" He took a last suck on the glass tube. "Hey, where are we going for dinner? I'm starved."

. . .

It was 2:30 a.m. Fran heard the girl go through the living room of the apartment and out the front door. She waited a few minutes until the car started and moved up the driveway onto the road. She walked into the living room. There was a lamp on by the card table in the corner. On the table was Baxter's briefcase. Fran opened it and sifted through the papers inside. There was a program from the Indy 500, some media plan recommendations from the agency, several newsletters from brokerage firms. Other than that just a few business cards, pads of paper and pencils. Nothing else, nothing useful. Fran let out a deep breath, sat down at the table, her head in her hands. There had to be a way to get him.

• • •

DAY 5

Burns & Cody

"Tonight, we have to agree on everything that must be done for the presentation. We have five days left. There won't be any time for revisions under the tight schedule we have. So, let's get ... " O'Brien jerked his head toward a sound at the back of the conference room. The people in the room turned away from O'Brien to see Clay Walker enter. They thought that Clay was out sick with the flu. Only O'Brien knew what had happened to him. Clay looked ashen, unsteady. He sat in the last row, waved at O'Brien.

O'Brien went on. "I've asked Sandy to take us through the work. You all know that she's been in charge of the creative during the last month. As it turned out, both the theme line for the campaign and the key visual treatment of it were her ideas." There was a buzz in the jammed conference room as Sandy got up.

"Most of you have heard the theme line, I believe." She held up a large, three by six foot rectangular board. "This is the key visual which we'll be presenting." On the left side of the board the letter "G" was emblazoned onto the familiar Global logo, a replica of the earth. Beginning with the "G", each of the letters became larger as the words "Going Your Way" were spelled out across the length of the board. As the words expanded, a series of lines extending from the globe stretched across the board. The lines were in the Global blue color, and as they lengthened in an expanding way, the visual emitted a strong feeling of flight. The visual had been accomplished with the help of the latest computer graphics.

O'Brien interrupted. "We think the total visual effect is unique and dramatic." There were a number of complimentary exclamations from the audience.

Sandy put the board aside. "We plan to interpret the words, 'Going Your Way' in three fundamental ways and we're going to make one prototypical commercial for each interpretation. The first idea inherent to the theme line is that Global can take you from wherever you are to anywhere you want to be. The airline serves 124 destinations so it's a supportable and believable promise. To make the point, we've selected a small destination, Hyannis, up on the Cape, rather than an obvious place like New York or L.A. I've got stats of the storyboard for this commercial for all of you. I won't take you through all the copy, but I will read you the core copy which will be in everything we do."

Wherever you're going,
Whenever you're going,
Whatever you say
We're Global Airways
Going your way.

"Now, let me explain something. You may have noticed I said 'Global Airways,' not 'Global Airlines.' Every carrier calls itself an airline, so we think changing to airways will stand out, plus there are a lot of tie-in possibilities between the word "way" in the theme line and the "way" in the new name.

"An idea we have is to use Charles Kurault as our announcer for television and radio. We're trying to contact him in the hope that we can record him tomorrow night, so make sure all the broadcast copy is with Dennis before that. The campaign slogan ties in with Kurault's reporting method, being on the road, travelling, and so forth. His voice, face, and demeanor are perfect for the new campaign's tone and attitude.

"The second commercial plays on the theme in the sense that Global understands your "way" of vacationing. Global has the places, hotels, condos, prices, rental cars, flights — the complete vacation from A to Z. This is supported by the enormous number of vacation packages that Global has put together. In this case, the prototype we've selected is a middle-aged couple getting away to Bermuda. The commercial takes them from the doorway of their home all the way through a complete Bermuda vacation experience. We're casting today and leaving Thursday. Fortunately, we've got Henry Bianchi as director for this. The film, or rather the tape, will be great. We don't have time to develop film, much less edit it. We're going to break every timetable record there is for all this work.

"The third commercial idea is to translate 'Going Your Way' into the flight experience itself. We didn't want to use the same old stereotypes that Americans have seen so many times before, smiling stewardesses and pilots, for example. It seems that Global is making some changes, some big and some small. Taken as a group, they should have a positive effect on the in-flight service. They effect seating, food and employee morale. In seating, they're going to take seats out of every plane so that the planes will be roomier than any other airline. Second, they've contracted with the best restaurants in the country to provide food on many flights.

The most interesting possibility in the in-flight area is employee morale. You've read about all the financial problems Global's been having, all the talk about takeovers and mergers. Naturally, that hasn't been good for the morale of their employees. It hasn't been good for flyers either because financial troubles spell worse service in the minds of flyers. So, Global's come up with a unique program. First, every employee gets five shares of stock free. Next, for every additional share an employee buys, the company gives the employee a free option for one year to buy another share at the same price. So, if an employee buys a share, at say twelve dollars today, over the next year he or she can buy another share at the same price. It's only a good idea if the stock goes up, but it doesn't cost the employee anything for the option and they're all getting five shares free anyway.

"Out of these changes we've created a commercial which will involve a range of Global employees, twenty or so, in very candid situations. Our plan is to get them to react to the news about the new seating, food and stock programs. Since the first they'll be hearing about of any of them will be from us we should get some real surprised reactions, and good ones, too. We have a production crew going to LaGuardia this afternoon.

"There's also a range of magazine, newspaper, and outdoor ads that will go with the commercials. We need to finish everything in time for the rehearsal the night before the presentation. Any questions? If not, good luck."

In the shuffle of everyone leaving the room, O'Brien took Sandy's arm. "Great job, that was a good rehearsal for the real thing. Just the right blend of enthusiasm and sincerity." As they approached the back of the room, Clay stood up.

"Sorry I was late. I got stuck in the tunnel. I've been writing my strategic part, Dennis, but it needs some work. But, tell me about the production schedule. You wanted me to supervise one of the shoots."

O'Brien looked at Sandy. "Right, Clay, that's right, but I didn't think you'd be back so soon, Sandy's been in charge. What's the latest, Sandy?"

"They could only shoot interiors today. There's been a lot of fog in Hyannis. McCloskey's in charge, but he hasn't done too many spots like this one."

Clay looked at O'Brien. "Good, I'll grab a plane in the morning and get up there. Sandy, which spot are you doing?"

"I leave for Bermuda tomorrow. All the pre-production has been done. No problems. It should be a great spot."

O'Brien leaned toward Clay. "You made a miracle recovery, didn't you?" He turned to Sandy. "Sandy, I'd like to spend some time with Clay getting him up to speed. Good luck in Bermuda. Please call me every day to let me know how it's going. That spot is the most important of the three."

"I'll keep you up to date. We should have it in the can by Monday, ready for the rehearsal on Tuesday. Say, I better get going. I'll talk to you later."

O'Brien waited for Sandy to leave the conference room. "What the hell is this, you're supposed to be in the hospital, on your way to ... "

"That's true, but they were so pleased with my progress they said I could go back to work."

"What? You told me you were looking at thirty days of rehab." He looked around to make sure no one could have heard him.

"They told me now that I'm clean it was O.K. if I came back to work and did the rehab later, you know, next week."

"Look, it sounds like baloney to me. You look lousy."

"You should have seen me a few hours ago. I'm getting stronger by the minute. The bastards drugged me, damned near killed me."

"I know your game, and I'm willing to go along provided you don't kill yourself. I can't imagine, now that you're not drinking, that a few days work will harm you. But, one promise."

"What's that?"

"That you follow their orders after this is over, win or lose. Deal?"

"Deal."

"O.K., I hope I don't regret this."

"You won't. Now, give me the details of what you want me to do."

"Come on, we'll go to my office." He led Clay from the room. "You really are nuts, you know."

• • •

DAY 4

LaGuardia Airport

"Global Airlines announces the delayed departure of flight 4633 to Hyannis due to fog in the arrival area. The new departure time is 9:15 a.m."

Clay Walker slumped into a seat halfway down the concourse to his departure gate, grateful for the extra time. His head was clear, but he felt weak, bone weary. Was this the after effects of what they had given him in the hospital or did he still have the flu? He couldn't tell. As bad as he felt, he was at least free of the hospital and the rehab unit.

He could see an airport bar from where he sat. There were just a few scattered customers, solitary drinkers. Were they drinking because of their fear of flying or was it something more familiar to Clay, a need for a pick me up? He had never had a drink in the morning until that day in Grand Central. Did it mean that he had a problem, as the hospital people, and even his family, believed? Or, was that just a one-time event brought on by his circumstance that morning? Today, just the thought of a drink made him feel worse.

He opened his briefcase and took out the photostat of the Cape Cod commercial. He recalled Sandy saying the idea was to demonstrate that Global flew everywhere, no matter where you lived or where you were going. Hyannis, as a tiny airport, was the acid test of this universality. The first two frames of the storyboard showed wide shots of the small town. Next, there were shots of the outside and inside of the little terminal. A single plane was shown approaching the airport, landing and taxiing up to the terminal. There was a scene of a small group of people greeting an equally small group of passengers leaving the plane. The final scene showed the new Global logo graphically transforming itself into the "Going Your Way" theme, much like the visual Sandy had shown at the copy meeting.

"Global Airlines announces that flight 4633 to Hyannis is now ready for boarding."

Clay got up, moved slowly the remaining distance to the flight, joined a handful of people queuing at the gate. He glanced back toward the main terminal. Two middle aged men stood out. Both were out of shape, pale, yet dressed as outdoorsmen. Boots, outsized backpacks and heavy hats made them seem out of place as they trudged along. Then, he recognized Steve Sparrow and one of the agency's lawyers. It was the first group from the agency headed to Outward Bound. He turned his head, avoided them, got on the plane.

. . .

Hyannis

"You were lucky to land here today, Mr. Walker. Most flights into Hyannis were canceled. We've had fog all week. In fact, all spring. Warm days, cool nights will do it every time."

Clay got into the taxi, leaned back, closed his eyes. "They told me the motel is pretty close to the airport."

"It's right across the airfield, only we have to drive all the way around to get there." He eyed Clay through the rear view mirror. "What brings you to the Cape?"

Clay didn't feel much like talking. "I'm with an advertising agency, we're making a commercial around here."

"Oh, you're part of that group. Everybody in town knows about them. We don't get that kind of excitement every day. Your friends have taken over the airport. The fog hasn't helped, they haven't been able to shoot outside at all, just a lot of inside stuff."

The car wound its way around the curved road. "Look at this, it's gotten worse since you landed. This is thick." He slowed the car.

As they came around a sharp turn in the road Clay saw a flash of light to the right. There was a sound, as if someone had exploded some fireworks, followed by a second flash of light, then a louder, closer noise. A shining object appeared to be coming directly toward them. "Pull over, quick." As the driver obeyed, Clay saw it, a small plane cartwheeling through the woods just above the road. There were sounds of tree limbs breaking and falling, a loud thud, then silence. Smoke rose in the woods a hundred yards from the car.

Clay jumped out.

"Hey, Mister, what are you doing? Where are you going? There's a lot of smoke up there. Stay away."

Stumbling, waving his arms in front of him, Clay pushed his way through the brush toward the smoke. At a clearing, he could see the plane sitting on its side, leaning against a lone tree, one wing in the air. The pilot's door had been thrown open so that the pilot, held by his seat belt, hung halfway out of the plane. Clay could see the man was unconscious and alone. A large cut bled from above his eyes. Standing on a nearby rock, Clay tried several times to climb onto the plane, each time slipping and falling to the ground. He stood again, reaching up to the pilot's hanging arm. Pulling on the arm, he dislodged the man enough to grab his shoulder. In a desperate tug, Clay's feet left the ground as the man became free of the plane and fell directly onto him. The increasing smoke from the plane's engine blew across them, causing him to gasp for breath. He could barely see.

The man was a dead weight on top of him. Pushing with both arms, Clay rolled the man off, away from the plane. Standing and leaning over, he found the man too heavy to drag. Clay lay down once more against the man. Using all his strength, he pulled the man onto himself and rolled him over, away from the plane. He repeated the maneuver again, then again, under him, pushing and rolling as in a child's game, finally falling and pitching together down a fifty foot slope into a ravine, as a bright light flashed and the plane exploded.

• • •

DAY 3

Aboard Global Flight #265

Murphy barely had time to pick up the paper before he boarded the flight. He was the last person on before they shut the door. The girl came over. "Orange juice, champagne, or half and half?"

"Just some juice, thanks." He caught his breath, opened the newspaper. Each day since he had purchased the Global options, he had gotten into the habit of buying the *Wall Street Journal.* He pored over the paper, page by page, seeking the news that would make him rich. The attendant returned with the glass of juice. There was nothing on the first page. He turned to the part of the paper which had news about mergers and acquisitions. "What's this?" he said out loud. The headline knocked the wind out of him. "Carrier Denies Tender." He read on.

> A spokesman for American Airlines put to rest today the rumors about a tender offer for Global Airlines. Philip Ross, Director of Public Relations, said that there was no truth to the

> Wall Street talk about American seeking control of Global, the financially ailing airline. A spokesman for Global confirmed that neither American nor any other airline had approached them about a possible takeover. Global's stock plunged on ...

His glass tipped, the juice splashing into his lap.

"Sir, are all right? Let me help you." She handed Murphy some towels. "Let me get some club soda. That's good for juice stains. Sir, are you O.K.? Shall I get the captain?"

Murphy dismissed her, huddled against the window. What was going on? He would be out the two-hundred thousand he had paid for the options. Yet, with two months left before they expired, surely something would happen. The article didn't represent what was really going on. That's what companies did, denied the truth, right up to the moment a takeover was announced. That had to be it. He had seen the memo, proof that something was in the works. The story in the paper was some kind of investment banker ruse to depress the stock just before the takeover. It would work out. He looked at the headline again and felt sick.

He had to clear his head. Today was one of the most important days in his life, a day he suddenly had mixed emotions about. His suitcase, under the plane, contained the hundred thousand dollar payoff to the girl. Her instructions to him were clear, to meet her at the bar at 10:00 a.m. No one would be there at that early hour. She would bring the proof of the demise of the Minister. Although he now had misgivings about the plan and the cost of it, it was too late to change. At least when it was done, he could put the Minister and his influence over him behind.

The hundred thousand for the girl, the two-hundred for the options, the fifty for Kreeger would put a big dent in his sign-up bonus at Comnet. But, he would still have a nice cushion, plus what he had in the bank. He could still buy the summer house. Besides, with his million dollar salary he could afford some big mortgages if necessary. He would be rich, even if the airline merger didn't take place.

"You look a lot better, Mr. Murphy." He settled into his seat, picked up the sports section of *USA TODAY.* It would be good to get back to some simple basketball bets when all of this was over.

. . .

San Sebastian

Murphy got there first. He took a seat against the mirrored wall, placed his case under his chair. The room was empty. He hoped she wouldn't keep him waiting. He felt uneasy, anxious to get off the island, away from this ugly affair. He would start fresh, block this whole business from his mind. He leaned forward, rubbed the back of his hand across his nose, waited.

A door opened across the room from Murphy, throwing a beam of outside light into his eyes. The glare from the door disguised the identity of the silhouetted figure entering the room.

"Regina, is that you?" The door shut. Murphy's eyes, then his mind searched to identify the figure, still hazy. "Regina?"

They saw each other in the same instant, with shared stares of amazement, just as the bar transformed into a cacophony of sound, twisting mirrors and blinding, flickering lights.

The sound of the first shot echoed behind Murphy before he saw the gleam from the pistol. Grasping under his chair, Murphy got his briefcase open, his 45 out. He stood up firing, the target moving now, an image bounced abruptly about by the rotating mirrors, strobing lights.

Both moving now, firing, lights and mirrors crackling, exploding from the flying metal, the music deafening. Murphy hit, feeling the sharp pain, lunging across the space at his assailant, falling into each other, then to the floor, gaping at each other in one last act of mutual enraged recognition. Then, silence. Lights unblinking. Mirrors still.

The girl emerged calmly from behind the bar. Idly, she stepped over the two sprawled men, first finding Murphy's case, then the other's. She walked from the bar, a case in each hand, smiling, confident, pleased with the complete success of her plan. After all, she had fulfilled the terms of her agreements with each of them. She deserved to be paid.

. . .

Bermuda

Technically, the Bermuda commercial was not complicated. It used the "eye of the camera" technique. Everything in the commercial was seen from the perspective of a vacationing couple. The technique allowed the camera to visualize the island, the local people, and the myriad activities available in Bermuda, all in a consistent manner and from the standpoint of the vacationers.

The weather in Bermuda had been in the agency's favor so that in two days and one evening enough tape had been recorded to make a commercial to everyone's satisfaction.

On Sunday evening, after all the work had been completed, the group decided to visit the Princess Hotel for dinner prior to catching the first plane to New York on Monday morning. The Princess, located at the tip of the island, was a large hotel, capable of handling meetings and conventions.

It was also a honeymoon favorite. As Sandy went into the lobby with the production crew there was a young couple holding hands by a fireplace. She stopped and stared across the room at them. She thought of her husband and the happy times they had enjoyed. She wondered if she would ever again have a life like that, someone to share with, someone to love.

A picture of O'Brien came to her: his curly hair, his look of confidence. His outspoken declaration of his love for her had taken her by surprise. She had been deeply touched. She thought about how she had come within an instant of giving herself to him in his office. How much of that desire was the need to fulfill a deep longing and how much of it was an unrecognized attraction to O'Brien? She could only say that if he was truly getting a divorce, then she would be willing to see him when the presentation was over. After that, who could tell what might happen?

The group took a large table in the lobby, where a cocktail waitress was available to get drinks from the main bar. "What a shoot, what weather. A little champagne is called for," said the film director, Henry Bianchi. "Let's have some Dom Perignon." The girl left to get the champagne and some glasses. Bianchi fished in his pocket and took out what appeared to Sandy at first glance to be a cigarette. Then she noticed the crimped ends, the uneven shape. Bianchi lit up, inhaling, holding his breath. He passed the smoking object across the table to the tape editor, who took a long drag, passed it back to Bianchi. The girl returned with a tray of glasses and two champagne bottles. From her seat Sandy could see the waitress noticed the distinct smell of the smoke.

The two bottles of champagne disappeared fast as they told stories and laughed at some of the unusual events during the shoot. Bianchi ordered two more bottles, took another stick from his pocket, lit it, and passed it around to his production crew members.

The police arrived simultaneously at the front and the back of the hotel. Whistles were blown, people shouted, fingers were pointed. They were surrounded. In no time a large Bermudian policeman had grabbed Henry Bianchi, handcuffed him. The management of the hotel was busy identifying the others. The police outnumbered the agency group two to one.

One of the cops grabbed for Sandy's arm. She spun away, jumped on a chair, sprung over it to the floor. She dashed fifteen yards across the lobby, hurdled a couch, dodged another cop and burst through two others blocking a doorway. She hit the swinging doors on the fly, entering what turned out to be the kitchen. Wending her way through an alarmed group of kitchen help, she found herself in the linen storage area. Spying two following police, she darted up a corridor, down a flight of steps into the garage at the back of the hotel. She sprinted through the garage out into the parking area, down the hotel driveway to a larger lot, where she had parked her motorbike. She aimed it down the hill, past the hotel toward the main road. She could hear the noise of the commotion at the front of the building. Lights flashed behind her.

It took Sandy ten minutes to ride back to her hotel, enough time to analyze what was happening. First, it was unlikely that anyone else had gotten away. All of them would have been arrested. Second, the Bermudian officials would take what had happened very seriously. The peacefulness and beauty of the island belied the strict, almost military police influence. Drugs were taboo. Bermudians knew that any disruption to the serenity of the island, particularly if it became publicized, could undermine the island's only industry, tourism. Third, it would not take the police long to determine what hotel the agency group was staying at. They would be coming fast to look for her and to confiscate the group's belongings, including the videotape. It was clear to Sandy that somehow, whatever it took, she must get the tape and get off the island immediately.

"I'm Mrs. Bianchi. Could I please have our key?" Sandy was nonchalant to the friendly clerk behind the desk at the hotel. "I think it's room 232, but you'd better look it up. We just checked in."

She went straight to Bianchi's room, found the tape in the special director's case he carried for that purpose. It took her less than five minutes to go to her own room and pack her shoulder bag. Retreating down the back steps of the hotel to the rear parking lot, she signaled a taxi that stood waiting at the front of a line. It would take fifteen minutes to get to the airport.

Sandy knew there were no scheduled flights to New York that evening. She had tried to leave at the end of the shoot that afternoon. She doubted, since there was no service to New York, that there would be a flight to any other U.S. city. It was close to midnight.

The bar at the airport was empty except for what appeared to be a few employees having an after-work drink. Sandy ordered a club soda. "Tell me, is there anyway at all to get off the island tonight?"

"Well," smiled the bartender, "there's always Canadian Joe." He pointed down the end of the bar to a man in a Texas hat. "He'll take you anywhere, anytime if you've got the do-re-mi."

Sandy approached the lone man. Jeans and boots completed his cowboy look. He drank from a longed-neck beer bottle, smoked a cigarette. She explained her situation to him.

He peered at her from under his hat, took a long drag on the cigarette. "New York. Tonight? You're talking big dough. Ten thousand dollars."

"When can we leave? Will you take credit?"

"I'll take all the cash you've got, the rest's on credit as long as you've got lots of identification. I'll also take care of that Rolex until the dough clears. We leave now. You look like a lady in a hurry."

Sandy had never experienced a take-off like that. It was pitch black in the area of the landing field where Canadian Joe kept his twin engine Otter. Once inside the plane, Canadian Joe started the engines. He steered the plane straight ahead from where it was parked, not bothering to find a runway, increased speed until they were airborne, the lights of Bermuda fading to the rear. Sandy looked at the cockpit clock. It was less than an hour since she had left the Princess. She started to shake.

• • •

DAY 2

Burns & Cody

Sandy walked into her office, dropped into her chair. The ride in the little plane had been into a strong wind all the way to New York, two-and-one-half bumpy hours. She had slept off and on in her apartment, but was still tired. Her head throbbed. She found some aspirin in her desk drawer. She was too tired to walk to the water fountain down the hall. She placed an aspirin tablet at the back of her mouth, swallowed. The pill went down, leaving a strong, salty aftertaste.

Her voice mail light blinked. She pushed the button, leaned back with a pad and pencil. Mostly, the calls were related to the myriad final production aspects for the Global rehearsal. The last call stood out, an urgent message from Ben Barney.

She got the overseas operator, and after some delay heard Barney's voice.

"Ben, how's the balloon business? How are the Big Birds coming along? Is there a problem?"

"We're on schedule, Sandy. When we're finished we'll be able to string Big Birds between here and San Francisco. But, that's not why I've been trying to reach you."

"What's up?"

I received this strange phone call from a guy at the Comnet agency. They ordered a gigantic balloon of a 767, painted in the markings of Global Airlines. They wanted it right away, finished, shipped and inflated in New York for a presentation. They were willing to pay *mucho dinero* to get the job done. So, I thought, isn't that one of my buddy Sandy's accounts? Every time I've been at your agency I've seen Global ads all over the place. So, I said to myself, what the hell is going on here? I don't like the smell of it. Maybe these guys are trying to steal my buddy's account."

"Ben, you have no idea how valuable what you're telling me is. Tell me all about it. When and where will this balloon be in New York?"

. . .

O'Brien sat in his office, looked at the butcher sign with the large 2 on it. One way or another it would be over in two days. He went over his master list of commercials, ads, billboards and associated materials that would be needed for the rehearsal the next day.

His intercom buzzed.

"What is it, Evelyn?"

"It's Clay Walker, from Cape Cod, line three."

"Clay, what's happening up there? I haven't had a recent report. I heard the weather's been a problem, fog."

"That's true, but I haven't seen the production crew, I've been tied up in the hospital here."

"Your in the Hyannis Hospital? What the hell happened? You didn't ... "

"No, this has nothing to with booze. Wait till you hear this. I saved a guy from a crashed airplane. Here."

"A crash, I haven't heard about any crash. What crash were you in?"

"I wasn't in it, I saw it, a small plane crashed right in front of me when I was driving from the airport. I pulled this guy out of his plane just before it exploded."

"That's astonishing."

"I still can't believe it, myself. I'll tell you the whole story when I see you. But, listen to this. This is the interesting part. The guy's on the board of Global. His name's Richardson. This is the guy who's supposed to break a tie vote on the agency if it's needed."

"And you saved his life. He must love you."

"I guess he does. But, that doesn't mean he's going to vote for us."

"What do you mean?"

"I've been with him for the last hour, he's told me his whole story. He's an investment banker. He's very close to Swenson, knew him when he was at Citibank. They've done a lot of business together over the years. He's arranged a lot of big financings that Swenson's been involved with, both at Citibank and at the airline. He got on the board of Global mainly through the help of Swenson. They help each other all the time. They're thick as thieves."

"What are you telling me? Are you saying you saved a man's life and he's not going to help you, help us."

"I guess he feels he owes me the truth, but he flat out said he has to do what he has to do, that he could never go against Swenson. He said he'll figure out some way to thank me later. Really, that's what he said."

"The guy's corrupt and an ingrate."

"Not the way he tells it, he can't stop thanking me for what I did. The other thing is just part of business, he said. Like it's totally removed from the rest of life."

"How is he, and how are you?"

"He has a mild concussion and a bad cut on his forehead, but he'll be released tonight. He'll be able to make the meeting easily. By the way, you said there was no likelihood of a tie vote."

"I still think that's true. But, hold it, I've got another call. Let me know as soon as you have information about the shoot. I've got to go, Evelyn's waving both hands at me like a mad woman." He hung up.

"What going on, Evelyn?"

"It's a Mr. Irwin. He's got a hell of a story to tell, but I think you should hear it firsthand. He's married to Fran Irwin of Global. Pick up line two."

"Hello, Mr. Irwin."

"Mr. O'Brien, you don't know me, but I'm sure you've met my wife, Fran. She's head of sales promotion at the airline."

"I have, doesn't she work for Maynard Baxter?"

"That's right, in fact that's what this call's all about. Baxter's been arrested in San Sebastian on drug possession. They found some hash in his attaché case. Then, when they searched his luggage, they found fifty thousand in cash. You know it's against the law to carry that kind of money around on airplanes. He's in big trouble."

"What was he doing with that kind of money?"

"It will all come out, but I can tell you he is a bad man, dishonest, the devil himself."

"Mr. Irwin, why are you telling me all this?"

"Because this is very important to your agency. Fran, my wife, was also arrested. Not because she did anything illegal, but because she was travelling with Baxter. They're holding Fran, asking her questions."

"I'm not sure I get it."

"Here's the point. Wednesday's your presentation to Global. What you don't know is Maynard Baxter was not going to vote for you. He was going to vote for that other agency, for Comnet. He's ... "

"Other agency? I didn't know there was another agency. When ... ?"

"I think there's a lot you don't know, but believe me, Maynard Baxter's tied in with that Swenson, part of a plan to dump your agency. Fran's been telling me about it for weeks."

"What about Fran's vote?"

"That's just it. Baxter's been threatening Fran, saying that if she didn't vote with him and Swenson she'd be fired. Fran's life has been a living hell working for Baxter."

"You mean Fran wanted to vote for us?"

"She thought it was an injustice to fire you."

"And, now?"

"Now, don't you see, Baxter's in jail. There's no way he can be in New York for the presentation. He's finished, anyway. They'll put him away for a long time."

"And, Fran?"

"Like I said, Fran is in jail, too. But, she told me to tell you that she'll vote for you, but somebody's got to get her out of jail. Fran says that you have the Tourism account for the island so that you must know people, important people in the government. The point is, Fran didn't do anything wrong. If they want to question her they can do that later. But, if she's going to make your presentation she's got to get out of jail. Do you know the people on the island?"

"I do, some of them. I've certainly met them all. But, we have a man here, Malachy Murphy, who runs the Tourism account for the island, he knows everyone well. The Minister of Tourism is his close friend."

"Murphy, the man who used to run Global until recently? I've met him."

"Don't worry, I'll call Murphy right away. We'll get Fran out some way, I can promise you that."

"From what I know about the voting, Fran can make the difference. The way Fran figures it, if she doesn't make it, it's going to be a tie. I don't know what happens to you then."

"I do, and it's not good."

"I can't call Fran back, and she's used up her one call out."

"Don't worry, we'll get her out. Thanks for all the information. I'll thank you in person when this is over."

"Good luck, Mr. O'Brien."

O'Brien yelled to Evelyn, "Get Murphy! I think he's in San Sebastian. It's life or death that we find him. And, find Sandy."

"I'm found." Sandy stepped into his office. "I brought you the Bermuda commercial, you're going to love it. There's a good story that goes with it, which I'll tell you later. But, listen to this. You're not going to believe it. Did you know that Comnet was making a presentation?"

"Not until five minutes ago. What do you know?"

"I know I need a good Marine to help me on a reconnaissance mission. I'll explain it to you in the car. It's urgent that you come with me now. I'm parked in front of the agency."

"This is madness. Wait a minute, where are we going? Let me get my cellular phone. How long are we going to be gone? We've got to prepare for the presentation."

"This will take an hour or two. You've got plenty of time to get ready for the meeting. C'mon."

"Shit, excuse me. Evelyn, if you get Murphy, give him the cellular number. But, get him, that's number one." He followed Sandy as she ran toward the stairway.

. . .

Lexington Avenue

"Put on the sneakers, the ones in the back seat."

O'Brien looked back. "What the hell is this? Ski masks, black gloves, sneakers. Are we robbing a bank?"

"Something like that." She headed for the Midtown Tunnel, explaining Ben Barney's phone call. "So, you see, this is a mission to help put Comnet out of commission. I figured your Marine Corps experience would be valuable."

They came out of the tunnel on the Queens side. The phone rang as soon as they hit the open air.

"Dennis, it's me. Hold onto your hat, I've tracked down Murphy. He's dead, killed in a shoot out on the island. It's on all the media."

"What, dead?" They slowed for the toll booth. O'Brien ran down his window, bought a *Post.* "This is beyond my imagination!" He read the headline over the phone and to Sandy. 'Minister and Mad Ave Man in Mutual Murder.' This is page one, with a picture." There was a wide shot of the bar, the two men sprawled on the floor. "My God, Murphy's on the front page, dead!"

Sandy leaned over, "It can't be, Murphy dead. Let me see it, isn't the other guy the Minister, the one who was going to help us get Fran Irwin out of jail?"

"You're right. Evelyn, you've got to get hold of the Prime Minister of San Sebastian. I've met him several times over the years. He's our only chance to free Fran Irwin. Call me back."

. . .

LaGuardia

Ben had told Sandy the balloon would be at LaGuardia. Comnet was planning on moving it during the first agency presentation to a position just outside the meeting room. Ben explained that Comnet was going to expose the balloon during their meeting with the Global board. At a specified moment the window blinds in the presentation room would be drawn back, revealing the huge balloon of a Global 767. Then, the head of Comnet, Spiro Bates, on a prearranged signal, would release the balloon, which would soar off into the sky.

Sandy drove the car around the back of LaGuardia and pulled off the road into an empty lot across from Butler Aviation where the private planes were kept. They put on the ski masks and gloves. Sandy took two kitchen knives from the glove compartment.

O'Brien looked at her. "Are you sure this is a good idea?"

She pretended not to hear him. "C'mon, let's go."

They crossed the street to the airfield. A small fence separated them from the field. They were five-hundred yards from the Butler terminal. As they approached they could see the enormous balloon silhouetted against the sky. It was tethered to some posts, halfway between them and the terminal. They covered most of the distance to the balloon, arrived at a four foot embankment of earth fifty yards away. They were able to lie against the embankment and clearly see the ropes which held the inflatable in place.

"It's tied at both ends. We've got to cut the ropes at precisely the same instant to have the most time to get out of here. I've got five of three. Here, take my watch and set yours by it. At exactly five after three we cut the ropes. Which do you want, the front or the back?"

"I'll take the back."

"O.K., when the balloon goes, so do we. I'll see you back at the car. They should be so shocked by what's happening that we'll have time to disappear. I bet you never thought advertising could be so much fun, Dennis."

"So this is what the Corps trained me for. This should replace the Outward Bound trip, don't you think?"

They went over the embankment, crossed the remaining ground to the balloon. "Global Airlines" was clearly emblazoned across it. Ben had done a first rate job as usual. She could not see O'Brien from her position. The second hand came up. It was five after three.

The rope cut easily, the balloon leapt into the sky, soaring toward Shea Stadium. As she turned to run, she could see a group of men racing from the Butler building, shouting.

They never saw the balloon go out of sight. They were back in the car speeding toward the entrance to the Grand Central Parkway, roaring between gasps for breath.

• • •

DAY 1

San Sebastian

"You must have friends in high places, *Señora* Irwin. I do not remember someone leaving so soon under the circumstances. You must sign this paper saying you will return to the island to testify. Otherwise, you are free to go."

"Whatever you want me to sign, I'll sign. I've got to get to New York."

It was 9:00 a.m., the agency presentations were underway. There was a 9:15 flight to JFK. If she missed that, the next flight would get her to New York too late. The agency would be out. Swenson and Kreeger would have voted to change, Haps Corwin and Ted Crowther to keep the agency. A tie. From what Baxter had said, a tie was as good as a win. The director who would break the tie was in Swenson's pocket.

Fran was reminded of her lack of exercise in recent years. She had to cover several hundred yards down one concourse, take the tram to change concourses to get to the New York gate. As luck would have it, the gate was at the end of the second concourse. Her shoulder bag strap dug into her, her knees hurt. If her high school field hockey coach could see her now.

The door to the jetway was still open, but the crowded waiting area indicated a full plane. She avoided the ticket desk and the lines, sought out the supervisor. She was busy with an irate customer who had been bumped from the flight, which was clearly overbooked. Fran waited patiently for the supervisor to finish, then flashed her Global ID card. "Hi, I've never asked for a favor in my fifteen years with the airline, but you have to believe that it's absolutely essential that I make this flight. A hundred million dollars is in the balance."

The girl studied Fran and her ID, disappeared for a minute, returned with an envelope. "Stand behind the pillar over there so I can give you this. No one can know that you work for the airline. We'll have a riot on our hands."

"I owe you a big one. Anytime you want tickets to a big sporting event call me at headquarters. I won't forget. The Super Bowl, whatever, just let me know."

She settled herself in the last row of the plane, checked her watch again. If the plane got to New York on schedule it would be a quarter to noon. The agency presentations were to start at 8:00 a.m., each for two hours. They would begin the voting at noon. The problem she had to deal with was that the plane landed at JFK, but the meetings were at LaGuardia. By now, Swenson would know of Baxter's arrests. And her own. He would be assuming a split vote and would be anxious to hurry the voting. It was unlikely that Swenson could learn of Fran's release, arranged by the agency.

The anxieties of the past day had enervated her. She leaned back against the tiny airline pillow. She had not been able to sleep the night before for fear that her plan would not work, that it would backfire. The idea of putting the hash and the glass tube in Baxter's briefcase had been a good one. She had stuffed the incriminating material into one of the sleeves of the case so that it would not be visible if Baxter were to open it for any reason.

If Baxter had discovered the planted evidence before they left, it wouldn't take long for him to figure out how it got there. She would be fired on the spot.

Another fear was that the materials would not look suspicious to the reader of the X-Ray machine. She had contemplated tipping off security if necessary, but fortunately that had not been required. From the conversation of the security agents, the glass tube had been the give away. It must have been a shape they had been taught to investigate. The look on Baxter's face had been worth all the grief the bastard had given her over the years. Fran had turned away from the verbal onslaught and to avoid Baxter's eyes. She'd always been afraid of him. The security people had to restrain Baxter from physically attacking her.

She knew as a matter of course they would go through Baxter's baggage, find the large amount of cash, four to five times the legal limit. All hell would break loose. She hadn't bargained on her own incarceration, had figured she'd be free to get to New York with time to spare.

It was a stroke of luck to remember that Malachy Murphy worked on the Tourism business at the agency, that there would be high level connections between the agency and San Sebastian. Obviously, her husband had been successful in reaching Dennis O'Brien and the agency had taken it from there.

The flight attendant arrived at the back of the cabin with just a few remaining magazines and periodicals. "I only have the local Spanish newspaper, *Señora*." Before the paper was in Fran's hands she could identify the large picture of Murphy. "What's this ... *Homicido* ... is that murder?"

"You haven't heard, it's big news."

She was baffled. It took her a long time to fall asleep as she speculated on the why's and wherefore's of the double murder. Even with her limited Spanish, she could see the paper had surmised all sorts of evil motives. She wondered if Baxter and Murphy had ever had a connection. She couldn't figure out how she'd been released if Murphy was dead.

The plane got to the gate on schedule, a plus of traveling in the middle of the day. Fran caused a stir by rushing up the aisle to the front while the plane was still taxiing. She wanted to be the first one off the plane, and succeeded, followed by an outburst of complaints and curses from a number of the first class passengers.

In all her years with the airline she had never taken a helicopter between JFK and LaGuardia, was only vaguely aware of its location in the terminal. She ran up the jetway, Global I.D. thrust out before her, was greeted by an airline employee holding a sheet showing gate connections to other flights.

"LaGuardia ... helicopter?" she yelled on the run.

"Between gates 17 and 18 on the B concourse."

It was standard airline humor that connecting flights were never convenient when you were in a hurry, or had heavy luggage. Halfway down the concourse she broke into a sweat, her shoulders and knees began to ache. "Hey, would you get this to Lost and Found?" She dropped her shoulder bag at the feet of a gate attendant, flashed her Global ID card, didn't wait for a reply.

Even without the bag she was gasping for breath when she reached the helicopter gate. "You're lucky, lady, this chopper was supposed to leave ten minutes ago, but we held it because of traffic control."

It was exactly noon when the aircraft lifted off. It couldn't take more than five minutes in the air to LaGuardia, another five to the meeting room, one she was familiar with as a convenient meeting place at the airport.

It was 12:25 when she stumbled up the stairway, burst into the room. Bill Swenson, confident, stood at the end of the only table in the room. "Why, Fran, we were just about to vote, you're just in time."

. . .

Burns & Cody

OBrien guided her into his office. "There's never been a party like that, do you think?" He rocked on his feet.

"Listen to it, the whole building is shaking." She watched him. "Dennis, I believe you're wasted."

"I'm not much of a drinker, you know."

"I'm convinced."

"Actually, I'm a lover." He pulled her against him.

"Is that right? The last time this happened you got into trouble." She got away from him.

"Just a guy expressing his love." He caught up with her, kissed her. She didn't resist.

"You know, Dennis, I could get you fired for sexual harassment, even if you are the damned president of the agency." She put her arms around him. They moved together in baby steps across the office, fell into the hammock, laughing.

"Do you have any experience with this?"

"Some, but it's been a while. I have a son, you know."

"I meant with the hammock, dummy."

"Oh, no. I'm not sure anyone has." He pulled her near him. "This could be a first."

"It is for me. I hope you're up to it."

• • •

EPILOGUE

P.J.'s

Clay wondered why he hadn't thought of it a long time ago, it was so simple. Vodka and orange juice. He watched for Yogi's signal, one finger, nodded his approval. Behind Yogi, he could see O'Brien heading toward the booth.

"Dennis, how does it feel to be president and have half the agency out of work with hangovers?"

O'Brien slid into the booth. "I sympathize with them, I don't feel that great, myself."

"It seems to me you left the main party rather early. It also seems to me you had a beautiful, blonde, about 5' 4", mini skirt, in tow. Would you like to comment on that?"

"I am nuts about her, you know."

"Is there anything you want to tell me?"

"I can tell you that she's going to replace me as creative director."

"Well done, an excellent first decision. You know, Dennis, I've been in a lot of major client meetings, new business shoot outs, you name it, but Sandy's performance was a *tour de force.*"

"I kept watching Swenson. He was totally taken by her, even though he knew he was going to vote against us."

The waitress arrived. "Orange juice for Mr. Walker, Lite Beer for Mr. O'Brien."

O'Brien studied Clay's drink. "Orange juice?"

"Yes, it's healthy, vitamin C, you know ... But, Sandy, she was dazzling, completely turned on, wire to wire. She lit up the room."

"How about Haps Corwin and Ted Crowther standing and applauding when she finished?"

"Yeah, and when Kreeger jumped up with them, Swenson had to grab him by his belt to put his ass back in his seat."

"The board member, your buddy, Richardson, was even caught up with Sandy. Is he taking you flying as your reward for saving his life?"

"He's invited me to go quail shooting."

"Wait till he sees you in your Marine fatigues with an automatic rifle. I wonder if he would have voted for us if he'd had a chance to vote."

"No fucking way, believe me, Dennis, he and Swenson are in cahoots."

"Poor Swenson, they say when Fran voted for us he completely lost it, had to grab the table for support."

"She's the hero of this piece, Dennis."

"I agree. From what I've learned, Maynard Baxter was a big time bad guy, involved in a lot of ugly stuff. He's history."

"Not as much history as Murphy. Can you believe it?"

"We don't know what the story was with him and the Minister, there's a lot of speculation, but no evidence. We do know he tried to pawn himself off on Comnet, and he tried to bribe Kreeger."

"You're kidding?"

"Spiro Bates called to congratulate us and told me that Murphy tried to sell himself to Comnet with a guarantee that they would get the account. Then, Kreeger was supposed to insist that Comnet hire Murphy for the Global account."

"It sounds like Murphy didn't think his career at Burns & Cody was bright."

"And after the chairman told him he was safe at the agency, that he would get other accounts to run."

"Dennis, did you talk to Murphy's wife?"

"Yeah, Maureen. She heard about what happened on TV. She was devastated."

"Will she be O.K.?"

"More than O.K. His life insurance policy at the agency doubles because he was on company business. That's a million dollars. Then, he had a good piece of Burns & Cody stock, plus some other investments, including part of a condo complex in San Sebastian."

"Really? Sounds like she's very well off."

"A lot better off than Steve Sparrow."

"I heard. How bad was his heart attack?"

"Serious, plus he was on the side of a mountain when it happened. He fell into a ravine, was broken up pretty badly."

"Well, at least he got the Outward Bound program canceled for the rest of us, something we couldn't do. Anyway, all's well that end's well."

"Aha, that's definitely Shakespeare."

"Hey, you're getting pretty good at this game."

"Here's your orange juice, Mr. Walker." The waitress smiled at Clay.

"How much of that can you stomach?"

"My doctor recommended it. You know, because of the flu."

"Speaking of doctors, when are you going to rehab? Remember, we made a deal."

"Well, we will be scheduling it, depending on the tests."

"Tests, what tests?"

"It seems there's a good chance that what they thought was a convulsion was actually a reaction to the flu."

"What?" O'Brien stared at him.

"Yeah, there was an article about this in the *Wall Street Journal.* False diagnosis. Apparently, there's a lot of confusion, people being treated for the wrong things. You can't be too careful."

"The *Wall Street Journal*?"

"Front page. You should read it now that you're president. Get rid of *Variety*, that sort of thing ... But, I want to hear about Sandy, was there heavy breathing?"

"Look, I told you how I feel about her."

"*Veni, vidi, vici*, I suppose. You don't have to tell me. Which reminds me, it's dark out there. You don't happen to have any change, do you? I need to make a phone call."

"Why do I have the impression you haven't changed?"

Clay got up. "I have. I'm running the biggest account at Burns & Cody and I report directly to the president of the agency." He smiled at O'Brien, got up, headed for the phones.

• • •